GUIDE TO NORTHERN CALIFORNIA

TO OUR READERS

Welcome to the new *AM/PM* Guide. Whether you're visiting, newly relocated or happily residing in Northern California, *AM/PM* can help you enjoy San Francisco and its nearby getaways to the fullest.

AM/PM's easy-to-carry format and comprehensive listings have inspired confidence for more than a decade. We do our homework, and we don't cut corners on quality. Our commitment to excellence means we stay on top of what's happening in Northern California.

You'll find some exciting new features in this *AM/PM*: introductions by well-known personalities, a California wine section with tasting notes by Master Sommeliers, calendars of interesting monthly events, children's activities, sports and much more.

With this edition, guests in Northern California's best hotels and resorts now have access to hardcover copies of *AM/PM* in their rooms. And businesses are using our corporate customized covers to say "welcome to San Francisco" in a uniquely personal way.

Trust *AM/PM* to show you what's best in San Francisco and Northern California. Use it, share it with your friends, and don't forget to tell our advertisers that you saw them in *AM/PM!*

THE PUBLISHERS

INTERIORS

HEALTH & BEAUTY

MARIN

**PLEASE FLIP BOOK OVER
FOR PM CONTENTS**

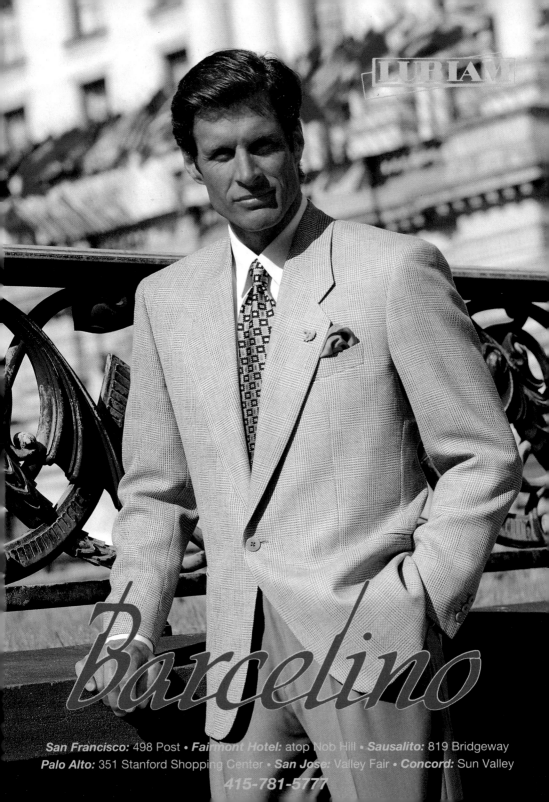

GUIDE TO NORTHERN CALIFORNIA

Publisher
ANA GLORIA HUSON

Co-Publisher
THIERRY ABEL

Associate Publishers
ANTHONY KALK   DAVID CLARIDGE

Editors
DONNALI FIFIELD   MAIA MADDEN

Production Manager/Wine Coordinator
CAROLYN DURYEA

Wine Editor
EVAN GOLDSTEIN

Design Director
MATTHEW FOSTER

Design Associates
RAOUL OLLMAN   JENNIFER T. POOLE

Photographer
JOSHUA ETS-HOKIN

Circulation Director
ROLANDO RODRIGUEZ

Director of Sales & Marketing
CAROLINE LARROUILH

Advertising Sales Executives
MADELINE AUSTIN   JAMES CASSADY

Business Manager
JENNIFER BAILEY

Interns
**BRADFORD CLARK   STEPHANE DEMILLY   JEROME BOESCH
SANDRINE CHORRO   MARC RIVOLLANT**

Published By:
AM/PM Publishing, Inc.
3027 Fillmore Street • Suite D • San Francisco, CA 94123
TEL: 415-921-2676 FAX: 415-921-3999
COPYRIGHT © 1993

ATTRACTIONS

SHOPPING

INTERIORS

HEALTH & BEAUTY

MARIN

SAN FRANCISCO IS CABLE CARS, THE GOLDEN GATE BRIDGE, SAILBOATS ON THE BAY, fog horns calling in the night. It's romance and history, a city of dreams, a magical place people yearn to

Attractions

visit. When they do, the magic is still here, waiting to cast its spell.

Getting around San Francisco is so easy that you'll soon discover the city's charms. Visitors from everywhere come to Union Square to shop because the world's most glamorous stores are in one compact area. You can walk to North Beach for coffee, explore the streets of Chinatown, picnic in Golden Gate Park, eat crab on Fisherman's Wharf — all in the same day.

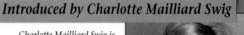

If you have just a day to see the sights, here's a tour that always pleases my guests, from friends to visiting heads of state. We start at the Golden Gate Bridge, crossing over to Vista Point to look back at San Francisco, crisp, clean and beautiful. I take them for a cable car ride, which makes even the most serious diplomat as giddy as a child. We walk through Chinatown, visit the stores around Union Square, and join the crowds on Fisherman's Wharf. We stroll through Golden Gate Park, one of the largest and

Introduced by Charlotte Mailliard Swig

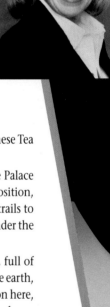

Charlotte Mailliard Swig is director of special events for the City and County of San Francisco and co-chair of San Francisco Clean City Coalition. The Coalition has united local civic groups, businesses and government to address litter and environmental problems and to ensure that San Francisco retains the charm and natural beauty that have made it famous.

loveliest city parks in the world, and linger in the delightful Japanese Tea Garden. Then, on to a museum, usually the nearby deYoung.

For a moment's reflection, no place is more majestic than the Palace of Fine Arts. Built for the 1915 Panama-Pacific International Exposition, it evokes San Francisco's romantic past. Wander down the little trails to the lagoon and watch the ducks glide gently through the water under the shadow of the graceful Palace columns.

San Francisco is like the world contained in 47 square miles, full of ethnic diversity and bustling with things to do and see. And like the earth, this city is a fragile community. Whether you live, work or vacation here, please do your part to keep San Francisco clean and litter-free. It belongs to all of us, and all of us need to cherish and respect it. That way we'll keep the magic, and those who come will continue to leave their hearts in San Francisco, always wishing to return.

Thank you: Joey Chase, Andy Marshall, Jennifer Wolf, EPIC Models

Henri Matisse, *Femme au chapeau*, 1905; SFMOMA, Elise S. Haas Collection

In 1905, Matisse's ***Woman with the Hat*** shocked the art world.
Almost a century later, she's still turning heads.
Visit her at the Modern.

SAN FRANCISCO MUSEUM OF MODERN ART

401 Van Ness Avenue at McAllister • 415/252-4000

VISITOR INFORMATION

SAN FRANCISCO VISITOR INFORMATION CENTER
900 Market Street..391-2000

RECORDED EVENTS INFORMATION
English 391-2001
French 391-2003
German...391-2004
Japanese...391-2101
Spanish 391-2122

EMERGENCY INFORMATION
Ambulance, Fire, Police...911
Coast Guard Search and Rescue 556-2103
Poison Control Center (24 hours a day)
....800-523-2222

If you have a medical emergency, you can contact the San Francisco Visitor Information Center at 391-2000 for a list of doctors and hospitals.

AREA CODES
San Francisco & Marin County.............................415
Oakland, Berkeley & East Bay..............................510
San Jose & Peninsula 408

HOTEL RESERVATION SERVICES
Bed & Breakfast International.............800-872-4500
Bed & Breakfast San Francisco 800-452-8249
Hotel Reservations Network 800-96-HOTEL

TIME & WEATHER
Time 767-8900
Weather...936-1212

San Francisco has a temperate, springlike climate year-round. Average temperatures range from 40 to 70 degrees Fahrenheit. The rainy season, with a light yearly rainfall, runs from November to April. In the summer, you will need a jacket for cool evenings and mornings when the fog rolls in.

FOREIGN VISITOR INFORMATION

CONSULATES
French 397-4330
German 775-1061
Japanese..777-3533
Spanish 922-2995

For other consulates, dial 411 for directory assistance.

CURRENCY EXCHANGE
American Express
237 Post Street 981-5533
For additional branches or to report a lost card, call 800-528-4800.

American Foreign Exchange Brokers
315 Sutter Street 391-9913

Bank of America
345 Montgomery Street 622-2451

Foreign Exchange Limited
415 Stockton Street 397-4700

Thomas Cook Currency Services
75 Geary Street..362-3452

Worldwide Foreign Exchange
150 Cyril Magnin. 392-7283

HELPFUL INFORMATION
Day-Owl Rexall Drug
159 O'Farrell Street......................................981-1090

United States Customs
555 Battery Street 705-4440

ATTRACTIONS

TRANSLATION SERVICES

Accredited Language Services...............800-755-5775
Alliance Francaise 775-7755
Berlitz Translation Services 986-6474
Japanese Language Services 296-9295

BAY AREA AIRPORTS

SAN FRANCISCO INTERNATIONAL AIRPORT

San Francisco International Airport is fourteen miles south of the city off Highway 101. The fifth-busiest airport in the country, SFO is in the midst of a three-year expansion program. For general airport information, call 876-7809. For information on short and long-term parking, call 877-0227. The airport is easily accessible. Driving to downtown San Francisco takes about 30 minutes. The airport is also well served by airport buses, taxicabs and car rental services to make your arrival in the Bay Area a pleasant one.

CAR RENTALS

Avis 877-6780
Budget Rent-A-Car..877-4415
Hertz 877-1600
National Car Rental 877-4745

LIMOUSINES

Associated Limousine...................................563-1000
Carey/Nob Hill Limousine & Tours 468-7550
Elite Limousine..421-2344
Gateway Limousine 510-829-0490
Ishi Limousine 567-4700
Limelite Livery 826-9630
Sedate Limousine...921-5377
Uptown Limousine 589-7373
Zephyr Limousine 564-3600

TAXICABS

You won't have trouble finding a taxi at the airport, but for your information there are more than 30 taxicab companies in San Francisco, most of them radio dispatched. The "big six" companies listed have the largest fleets, and offer speedy reliable service.

City 468-7200
DeSoto...673-1414
Luxor...282-4141
Pacific...776-7755
Veterans 552-1300
Yellow..626-2345

SUPERSHUTTLE

America's largest airport shuttle company offers door-to-door service to and from San Francisco Airport around-the-clock. Several hours' notice is required to take you to the airport 90 minutes before departure. Fare: $11 for adults, $8 for each additional passenger. Phone 558-8500.

AIRPORT BUSES

San Francisco International Airport is accessible via the *SFO Airporter*. Buses leave every 20 minutes from many San Francisco hotels and fare is $8 one way, $14 round trip. Call 495-8404. *SamTrans* provides inexpensive public bus service to the airport, picking up passengers at several stops along Mission Street downtown. Call 800-660-4287. From Marin County: *Marin Airporter* buses run regularly on the half hour, 461-4222. From the Peninsula: service is provided by two carriers, *SamTrans*, 800-660-4287, and *Airport Connection*, 363-1500.

OAKLAND INTERNATIONAL AIRPORT

Oakland International Airport, off Highway 880, serves Oakland and East Bay communities. You can get general airport information from 510-577-4000. Parking is usually plentiful; for rates, call 510-633-2571. The airport is minutes from downtown Oakland. The airport may also be reached by using the BART transit system. Get off at the Coliseum station for a ten-minute connecting bus ride to the airport. Airbart operates from 6AM-midnight, departing every ten minutes. Fares are $2. Access to San Francisco is easy. By car, the drive into the city takes 30-45 minutes. By BART, the ride is about 30 minutes. Airport shuttles also serve San Francisco and cities in the East Bay. For information, call 510-577-4015.

CAR RENTALS/OAKLAND AIRPORT

Budget Rent-A-Car 510-568-4771
Hertz 510-568-1177
National Car Rental 510-632-2225

SAN JOSE INTERNATIONAL AIRPORT

San Jose International Airport serves the booming communities in the Peninsula, south of San Francisco. Visitors to Stanford and the Silicon Valley may reach the airport via highways 101, 880 and 280. General information about the airport is available from 408-277-4759. For details on parking, call 408-293-6788. Numerous airport buses provide door-to-door transportation, including *Airport Connection* at 408-730-5555. Downtown San Jose is about ten minutes from the airport. To reach San Francisco, you can take the *VIP Airport Shuttle*, 408-378-8847. If you are driving, San Francisco is about an hour away via Highway 101 North.

CAR RENTALS/SAN JOSE AIRPORT

Avis :..408-993-2224
Budget Rent-A-Car 408-744-1930
Hertz 408-437-5700

AIRLINES

These are the major airlines serving the Bay Area:
Air Canada 800-776-3000
Air France 800-237-2747
Alaska 800-426-0333
American..800-433-7300
British Airways 800-247-9297
Canadian Airlines................................800-426-7000
Cathay Pacific......................................800-233-2742
China 391-3954
Continental...397-8818
Delta 552-5700
Japan 800-525-3663
Lufthansa 800-645-3880
Northwest 800-225-2525
Philippine Airlines 800-435-9725
Quantas 761-8000
Singapore 800-742-3333
TWA 864-5731
United 397-2100
USAir...800-428-4322

PUBLIC TRANSPORTATION

CABLE CARS

Cable cars are San Francisco's most distinctive form of public transportation. These cable cars, weighing six tons apiece, function by gripping the moving cable that runs below street level, then releasing it and braking to stop. Climb up quickly; the conductor will come around to collect your $3 fare. Phone 673-MUNI.

MUNI

The Municipal Railway (MUNI) crisscrosses San Francisco and is known as one of the nation's most convenient public transportation systems. Bus service on most lines is quick and competent, with an average wait of less than ten minutes. Fare for all buses and streetcars is $1; this includes a transfer good for travel in any direction for up to 1½ hours. Exact change is required. Fast Passes (monthly bus passes) are available for $32 at various outlets throughout the city. MUNI sells a map of its routes, available for $1.50 at newsstands. Phone 673-MUNI.

BART

Bay Area Rapid Transit (BART) is a modern transit system linking San Francisco with the East Bay, covering a distance of 71 miles. Trains run underground through the downtown region, travel an underwater transbay tube and rise to an elevated level throughout the East Bay. BART operates daily from 4AM to midnight Monday through Friday, 6AM to midnight Saturday, and 8AM to midnight Sunday. Ticket prices vary according to the length of your trip. SAVE YOUR TICKET, as you need it to exit the gates. Phone 788-BART.

ON THE BAY

One of the best ways to experience the beauty of San Francisco Bay is aboard the ferryboats, an integral part of daily life for transbay commuters before construction of the bridges in the 1930s. Today, they're still an extremely pleasant way to cross the bay, affording spectacular views of San Francisco, the Golden Gate and Alcatraz Island.

The Golden Gate Ferry operates from the Ferry Building on the Embarcadero at the foot of Market Street. Destinations are Sausalito and Larkspur Landing in Marin County. Adult fares are $3.75 daily to Sausalito; $2.50 weekdays, $3.25 weekends to Larkspur; children's fares are discounted. Phone 332-6600.

The Red & White Fleet whisks passengers from the city to Sausalito, Tiburon and Angel Island State Park, often via catamaran, departing from Pier 43½ at Fisherman's Wharf and from the Ferry Building on the Embarcadero at the foot of Market Street. Service to Marine World Africa USA and the Wine Country departs from Pier 41. Phone 546-2896.

EAST TO BERKELEY & OAKLAND

A/C Transit operates a bus service between San Francisco and Alameda and Contra Costa counties in the East Bay, primarily to Oakland and Berkeley. Buses traverse the Bay Bridge and depart from the Transbay Terminal at First and Mission streets. Phone 510-839-2882.

NORTH TO MARIN & SONOMA

Golden Gate Transit is a bus line linking San Francisco with Marin and Sonoma counties to the north via the Golden Gate Bridge. Buses depart from the Transbay Terminal at First and Mission downtown and pick up passengers at several stops in the city en route to the bridge, primarily along Van Ness Avenue and Lombard Street. Phone 332-6600.

SOUTH TO THE PENINSULA

SAMTrans (San Mateo County Transit District) offers bus service between San Francisco and communities along the Peninsula to the south, with Palo Alto as the southern terminus. Buses depart from several stops along Mission Street downtown. CalTrans operates CalTrain service from San Francisco to the communities of the Peninsula. The depot is located at Fourth and Townsend downtown. For information on both services, call 800-660-4287.

ALL ABOARD!

Amtrak service to Los Angeles and Seattle operates out of Oakland. Connecting buses leave San Francisco at regularly scheduled times from the Transbay Terminal at First and Mission downtown. Phone 800-872-7245.

DRIVING & PARKING IN SAN FRANCISCO

In San Francisco, you can turn right on red. While driving may be easy here, parking can be troublesome. Finding street parking will definitely make your day! Due to the city's vertical topography, local ordinances require curbing your wheels when parking on a hill. Turn your wheels toward the curb when parking downhill, away from the curb when parking uphill. Where street parking is unmetered, signs indicate time limits and street cleaning days. Curbs restrict parking as follows: **white curb** — passenger-loading zone; **green curb**—limited parking as posted; **yellow curb**—loading zone (commercial vehicles only); **red curb**—no parking; **blue curb**—handicapped parking only.

DRIVING INFORMATION

AAA..800-400-4222
California Highway Conditions...................557-3755

WEEKEND MECHANICS

Insta-Tune (Sat. only)................................775-4044
Lombard Tire & Brake (Sat. only)..............922-2808
Quality Tune-Up (Sat. & Sun).....................626-6446

TOURS OF THE CITY

NEIGHBORHOOD WALKING EXCURSIONS

Volunteers sponsored by The Friends of the San Francisco Public Library lead free tours of historic and architectural features of the city's neighborhoods. Most tours take 1½ hours and return near the starting point. No reservations are required. Groups of 15 or more must call at least six weeks in advance and school groups must have official confirmation so an additional guide can be scheduled. City Guides lead tours of Historic Market Street, City Hall, Nob Hill, Haight-Ashbury, Gold Rush City, the Fire Department Museum, North Beach, Coit Tower, Pacific Heights Mansions, Palace of Fine Arts, Victorian San Francisco, Cathedral Hill, Japantown, Presidio Museum and the Mission Murals: 557-4266.

FRIENDS OF RECREATION & PARKS

Free tours of Golden Gate Park are offered every weekend from May to October, rain or shine: East End, West End, Japanese Tea Garden, Lloyd Lake, Stern Grove and Strawberry Hill: 221-1311.

PERFORMING ARTS CENTER

Tours start at the Grove Street entrance to Davies Hall. Admission for adults $3, seniors and students $2. Call ahead since days and hours vary: 552-8338.

SPECIAL INTEREST TOURS

Dashiell Hammett Tour is a 16-year-old, four-hour walking tour exploring the San Francisco that detective novelist Dashiell Hammett wrote about. The tour leaves from the Main Branch of the Public Library, Larkin and McAllister, Saturdays at noon, May through August. Call first to confirm schedule: 707-939-1214.

Heritage Foundation offers a two-hour walk of the Victorian and Edwardian mansions of Pacific Heights, as well as specially scheduled tours: 441-3004.

Hidden Stairway Walks of San Francisco are conducted by Adah Bakalinsky, author of *Stairway Walks of San Francisco*. To reserve one of the 28 different two-hour walks, call at least three days ahead: 398-2907.

Near Escapes are off-the-beaten-track tours conducted several times a month and lasting two to four hours although some are all-day trips. Take part in The Great San Francisco Scavenger Hunt, tour a cemetery or the

HOW TO HELP KEEP SAN FRANCISCO ONE NEAT CITY

1. Have a fabulous time.

2. Don't litter.

The Clean City Coalition and the people of San Francisco
thank you.

PACIFIC ✶ TELESIS ℠
Group

People • Service • Environment
NORCAL WASTE SYSTEMS, INC.

Created by Young & Rubicam/SF

aquarium after hours. If solo tours are more to your liking, Near Escapes offers a drive-yourself tour of San Francisco and a walking tour of Chinatown, both on audio cassette: 386-8687.

3 Babes & A Bus takes you on a tour of San Francisco's nightclubs. The tour, given on Friday and Saturday nights, is a great way to get acquainted with the city's clubs and make friends while you party: 552-2582.

49 MILE DRIVE

Follow blue and white seagull signs for a pleasant 49 mile drive-yourself tour of San Francisco landmarks. The Civic Center, at the intersection of Hayes and Van Ness, is a good starting point. Some sights on the tour include the waterfront, Golden Gate Park and Ocean Beach.

BUS TOURS OF THE CITY

Gray Line Tours has been in operation in San Francisco for more than 80 years. Several different bus tours are offered, both day and night, at varying prices. A standard 3½ -hour city tour is $23.50, children from 5 to 11 are half price. Among their fleet are bright red British double deckers and motorized cable cars: 558-9400.

Cable Car Charters has a fleet of authentic cable cars restored and motorized for tours, conventions, shuttles, parties on wheels or promotions. Each cable car can accommodate 50 passengers (35 seated, 15 standing). Rates begin at $125 per hour: 922-2425.

SAN FRANCISCO BAY TOURS

The Blue & Gold Fleet departs from Pier 39, at the West Marina on Powell Street at the Embarcadero. Nowhere else on San Francisco Bay can you enjoy viewing the city skyline better than aboard the vessels of the Blue & Gold Fleet. This fully narrated 1¼-hour tour takes you through the picturesque landmarks of Coit Tower, Alcatraz and under both the Golden Gate Bridge and Bay Bridge. Departures are year-round. Enjoy a three-hour dinner dance or holiday cruise during the months of May through December. The cruise features a sumptuous buffet dinner and dancing to a live band. Reservations are required; major credit cards are accepted. Call 705-5444 for information. Blue & Gold also operates the Alameda/Oakland ferry with frequent departures seven days a week. Since the addition of the East Bay ferry, commuting has never been easier. For schedule information, call Ferryfone: 510-522-3300.

Hornblower Dining Yachts offers a unique view of the city. You can experience dining and entertainment from a different perspective — the bay. Weekend champagne brunches, elegant lunches and dinner dance cruises are available. Hornblower offers exciting entertainment for dancing, and the outer decks are perfect for strolling on a sunny day or starry night. You can also enjoy delicious buffets or seated meal service, featuring cuisine freshly prepared on board by Hornblower's talented chefs. Senior and group discounts are available, and private charters are offered: 394-8900, Ext. 7.

Pacific Marine Yacht Charters has four luxury motor yachts, including *The California Spirit* and *Pacific Spirit*, available to groups for private parties. A professional chef on board prepares gourmet meals. The charter service also arranges conference meetings, special events and wedding parties: 788-9100.

The Red & White Fleet leaving from Piers 41 and 43½ offers narrated tours of San Francisco Bay. Their boats cruise under the Golden Gate Bridge, and very close to infamous Alcatraz Island. Food and beverage service is available on board. Tours last about 45 minutes, with frequent daily departures: 546-2896.

ATTRACTIONS

FOR STREET MAP OF SAN FRANCISCO, SEE PULL-OUT MAP.

ALAMO SQUARE

San Francisco's celebrated "painted ladies" are between Hayes and Steiner streets in the Western Addition. The row of Victorian houses, which survived the 1906 earthquake, slopes up the hill. An impressive view of the city's skyscrapers makes this a favorite stop for pictures.

ALCATRAZ

Known as "The Rock," Alcatraz is really the Spanish word for pelican *(alcatraces)*. The island, originally a Civil War army fort, became a U.S. federal penitentiary in 1934. Surrounded by icy and treacherous currents, it maintained its reputation as "escape proof" until 1963. Now in ruins, the famous maximum security prison is a national park and a popular tourist attraction. The tour takes about 2-2½ hours. You can purchase a round-trip ticket from the Red & White Fleet at Pier 41 on Fisherman's Wharf. Be sure to wear comfortable walking shoes and a windbreaker. National Park Service rangers offer a walking tour of the island. An audiocassette tour of the cell house is also available.

ANGEL ISLAND

A perfect place to while away a sunny day, Angel Island State Park, hilly and blanketed with trees, is a pleasant contrast to Alcatraz. In the past, it has served as a military installation, prisoner-of-war camp and immigration center — when it was known as the Ellis Island of the West. Now, abundant wildlife, picnic areas, hiking and bicycling trails cover the island, making it a favorite ferry destination for locals and tourists alike.

SAN FRANCISCO WINE SHOPS

With Napa Valley and Sonoma County right next door—and with the number of new wineries in Monterey County, too—it's no surprise that San Francisco has a well-rounded list of wine shops to choose from:

CALIFORNIA WINE MERCHANT

3237 Pierce St. at Lombard / 567-0646

California wines are the specialty at this family-owned business. A newsletter and free local delivery are added attractions.
Open daily

DRAPER & ESQUIN

655 Davis St. at Pacific / 397-3797

Importing wines directly for more than 40 years, Draper & Esquin specializes in Burgundies and old and rare wines. Other features: a wide price range and bimonthly newsletter.
Closed Sunday

JOHN WALKER & CO.

175 Sutter St. at Montgomery / 986-2707

John Walker & Co. has offered fine wines and spirits since 1933, including French wines, rare California wines and liqueurs. Other services: wine storage, cellar appraisals, worldwide shipping, local delivery and complimentary gift wrapping.
Closed Sunday

PACIFIC WINE COMPANY

124 Spear St. at Mission / 896-5200

Pacific Wine's large selection includes small California cellars, French Burgundies and German wines. In business 13 years, the shop has a bimonthly newsletter and wine tastings, which make it a favorite of connoisseurs.
Closed Sunday

PLUMP JACK WINES

3201 Fillmore St. at Greenwich / 346-9870

This elegant store displays vintage Bordeaux, Burgundies and California wines, as well as an excellent selection of Champagnes, sparkling wines, Ports and dessert wines. Wine books and elegant gift baskets are also offered.
Open daily

THE WINE SHOP

2175 Chestnut St. at Pierce / 567-4725

Since 1968 the same owners have run this shop with its large choice of California and European wines. Offerings include nightly wine tastings, a monthly newsletter and a selection of glassware. Free local delivery with minimum orders.
Open daily

CHINATOWN

From the central downtown hotel and shopping district, it's just a short walk to Chinatown, one of the largest Chinese-American communities in the United States. **Grant Avenue** is a colorful patchwork of pagoda rooftops, carved wood detailing, dragons and Chinese lanterns. Bright souvenir shops sit alongside dignified stores offering intricately carved ivory, silk blouses, brocades and fine linen. **Stockton Street** offers a staggering variety of fresh seafood markets, herb shops and outdoor produce stands displaying exotic fare at reasonable prices. The air is filled with spicy aromas from restaurants, pastry shops and deli-style markets featuring roasted ducks, live chickens and a number of cooked delicacies to take home.

CIVIC CENTER

Renowned for its French-inspired Beaux Arts architecture, San Francisco's City Hall is the focus of the Civic Center, a handsome cluster of government and cultural institutions. The lofty dome at **City Hall** houses a beautiful rotunda and grand staircase, providing an elegant setting for stately functions. Across Van Ness Avenue, the classically designed **War Memorial Opera House** and **Veterans Building** contrast with **Davies Hall**, the modern performing arts center that is the home for the San Francisco Symphony. Another impressive structure in the Civic Center complex is the main branch of the San Francisco Public Library, completed in 1917. Parking is available beneath a tree-lined concourse. Nearby, the **Opera Plaza** residential and commercial complex has revitalized the entire area; many good restaurants have popped up all around the Civic Center.

FINANCIAL DISTRICT

"Wall Street of the West" aptly describes the businesslike side of San Francisco. Banks, brokerage firms and insurance companies crowd into a compact area of concrete and steel skyscrapers, where the sun rarely shines and bicycle messengers speed past alarmed pedestrians. The downtown Financial District is corporate headquarters for multinational conglomerates, and it's the home of the **Pacific Stock Exchange**. Visitors stand in awe of the **TransAmerica Pyramid**, which, when finished in 1972, caused an uproar due to its unusual shape. The Pyramid has since become a fondly regarded symbol. At 853 feet, it is San Francisco's tallest building. As imposing in its own statuesque way is the soaring 52-floor carnelian marble **Bank of America Center**, headquarters of the state's largest bank. In close proximity to the Financial District, the **Embarcadero Center** is crowded with shoppers during the week. The nearby **Hyatt Regency Hotel** is another striking architectural landmark noted for its dramatic atrium lobby, where bullet-shaped glass elevators whisk guests to their floors and to **The Equinox** at the top. This

revolving restaurant/cocktail lounge features a spectacular panoramic view as it turns 360 degrees every 45 minutes.

FISHERMAN'S WHARF

No visit to San Francisco is complete without at least one foray to the Wharf, now extending from Ghirardelli Square to Pier 39. Early morning is the best time to appreciate the maritime sights. Fishing boats leave as early as 4:30AM and hardy fishermen can be seen guzzling coffee around their heaters as the fleet heads out to sea. Streets lining the Wharf teem with souvenir shops, crab pots and sidewalk artists displaying their talent. Famous seafood restaurants offer a fresh catch-of-the-day along with local specialties of petrale sole, salmon and cioppino. **Pier 39**, built of weathered wood, is a two-level collection of specialty shops and restaurants overlooking the bay and a colorful marina. A variety of entertainment is provided daily for the many visitors, and children are thrilled by the merry-go-round and amusement center full of the latest video games. Friendly sea lions, sometimes as many as 300, beg for snacks thrown by tourists on the docks. In late 1994, Pier 39 will unveil Underwater World, revealing first-ever views of the bay and its inhabitants. **Ghirardelli Square** and **The Cannery** are handsomely designed shopping complexes renovated from a red brick chocolate factory and a Del Monte fruit processing plant, respectively. These two attractions feature boutiques, fine restaurants and specialty shops in pleasant surroundings. **Aquatic Park**, at the foot of Polk Street, provides a fishing pier for sportsmen.

FORT MASON CENTER

Formerly an army installation, Fort Mason was opened to the public in 1977 as a community-oriented complex offering free or low-cost activities. Situated on the waterfront at the eastern end of the Marina Green and yacht harbor, the fort's seven buildings and two piers house theatres, galleries, museums, classrooms and environmental organizations. The spacious piers at Fort Mason are used for a variety of exhibits, fairs and festivals. The **Jeremiah O'Brien**, the last World War II liberty ship in operating condition, is open to visitors daily from 9AM to 3PM at Pier 3.

FORT POINT NATIONAL HISTORIC SITE

Completed in 1861, Fort Point was established as the main defense structure of the military **Presidio**, an encampment to protect the entrance to San Francisco Bay. Its position on the Golden Gate headlands gave it a strategic overview. The fort was manned with two companies of the 3rd Artillery during the Civil War. Reputed to be the only brick seacoast fortress on the West Coast, Fort Point never saw action. On display in the museum are many of the cannons, swords, guns, military surgical instruments and uniforms of the period. Fort Point can

be reached via Lincoln Boulevard where signs mark the turnoff to the fort under the Golden Gate Bridge.

GOLDEN GATE BRIDGE

The most famous symbol of San Francisco, the bridge's dramatic single-span structure joins the city to Marin County across the gateway to San Francisco Bay. Designed to withstand hurricane-force winds and painted international orange to be visible in fog, the magnificent bridge was opened with fanfare on May 27, 1937. Its enduring beauty combines a spectacular setting with a graceful design. The bridge owes its existence mainly to chief engineer Joseph Strauss, who was ridiculed when he suggested bridging the gateway in 1918. By 1933, his idea was deemed feasible and the massive engineering project began, taking 4½ years to complete.

GOLDEN GATE NATIONAL RECREATION AREA

The Golden Gate National Recreation Area is the largest urban national park in the world — 28 miles of unspoiled shoreline extending northward to Pt. Reyes in Marin County. In San Francisco, the national recreation area encompasses **Ocean Beach, Land's End, Baker Beach, Crissy Field, Fort Mason Center, Fort Point National Historic Site, Aquatic Park** and the **Presidio**.

GOLDEN GATE PARK

Planning for San Francisco's largest park began in 1868. Thanks to the foresight of John McLaren, a Scottish gardener who became park superintendent, 1,017 acres of sand dunes were transformed for the use of all San Franciscans. Golden Gate Park, three miles long and half a mile wide, was landscaped to include an incredible variety of trees, shrubs and flowering plants. At the park's easternmost edge is the **Panhandle**, a green strip on which you can find some of the park's oldest trees. The park provides city dwellers with grassy picnic sites, wooded walking trails, a chain of lakes, and plenty of room for bicycling, skating, softball, horseback riding, tennis and golf. Row and paddleboats can be rented at Stow Lake. The **California Academy of Sciences** contains a fine aquarium, planetarium and natural history museum. Across the concourse, the **deYoung Museum**, the **Asian Art Museum** and the **Japanese Tea Garden** offer additional sights to savor. Other park attractions include **Strybing Arboretum** and **Botanical Gardens, Rhododendron Dell, Shakespeare Garden**, a buffalo paddock, polo field, children's playground and carousel. Also, look for the elegant glass **Conservatory of Flowers**, brought around the Horn to be assembled piece by fragile piece in Golden Gate Park in 1878. A wild and forbidding tangle of wind-twisted cypress and eucalyptus trees greets the explorer of **Land's End**. This remote stretch of seacoast is located along the northwestern edge of **Lincoln Park**, where ocean meets coastline with a blast of windy fury. Hikers in this desolate

DISCOVER

THE CALIFORNIA ACADEMY OF SCIENCES

STEINHART AQUARIUM
MORRISON PLANETARIUM
NATURAL HISTORY MUSEUM

IN GOLDEN GATE PARK

OPEN EVERY DAY, 10 AM TO 5 PM
FOR INFORMATION CALL 415/750-7145

ATTRACTIONS

CHINATOWN

by Tommy Toy

The fierce dragons and stone lions guarding the "gateway to Chinatown" at Bush and Grant usher visitors into a truly foreign community. Vibrant colors and exotic scents fill the streets, which bustle with curious tourists and Chinese residents of all ages. As you explore the 24-block area of San Francisco's Chinatown, you will discover a neighborhood unlike any other in the city.

Shops line Grant Avenue, offering everything from fabrics, pottery and furniture to jewelry, cameras and memorabilia — often at bargain prices. Try Chong Imports (838 Grant) for a variety of souvenirs and groceries. Antique lovers will appreciate the museum-like interiors of Dragon House (315 Grant) and D. Wong's (338 Grant) and their collections of Chinese carved wood furniture and delicate pottery.

When walking the streets of Chinatown, take note of the carved cornices and flowered balconies on many of the buildings. The Bank of America building (701 Grant) is a good example, with ornate columns and dragons enlivening its facade. You'll see Chinese characters and ornamentation everywhere, even on the telephone booths and street lights along Grant.

To uncover the real Chinatown, wander down its alleys and side streets. It is there that the echoes of an ancient and fascinating culture resound.

Tommy Toy owns two of Chinatown's best restaurants. The Imperial Palace (919 Grant) offers authentic, award-winning Chinese cuisine in an opulent setting. Tommy Toy's Cuisine Chinoise (655 Montgomery) is renowned for its delicate blend of Chinese flavors with a French flair.

landscape are cautioned to stay on the trails, as unwary visitors have been swept from the rocks and drowned. Picnic tables are available on the **Sutro Heights** side of Lincoln Park overlooking the Pacific. Sea lions on **Seal Rock** entertain visitors to the **Cliff House**, a popular restaurant and bar perched over the restless surf. Huge windows give each guest an uninterrupted view of magnificent sunsets. On a clear day you can see the Farallones, a chain of islands 26 miles from shore, populated only by sea lions and birds.

HAIGHT-ASHBURY

Near Golden Gate Park, Haight-Ashbury is a district of Victorian houses immortalized in the 1960s as the home of the flower children. The Haight is still a vibrant community. Haight Street has a wide variety of cafes and boutiques, including tie-dye shops and interesting gift stores. The intersection of Haight and Ashbury, for which the neighborhood is named, is in the middle of the commercial center.

JACKSON SQUARE

Jackson Square is a picturesque and historic quarter of San Francisco where you'll discover many of the city's oldest remaining buildings. Due to their sturdy construction of brick and stone, the structures miraculously survived the earthquake and fire of 1906; the heavy iron shutters effectively served as fireproofing. The Gold Rush of 1849 attracted hordes of prospectors who, anxious to stake their claims in the gold country, abandoned their ships at anchor in San Francisco Bay. Many of these hundreds of ships, falling into disrepair, were sunk and filled, which extended the city's shoreline eastward from **Montgomery Street.** It's fascinating to note that a good number of the brick buildings in Jackson Square have sailing vessels as foundations and walls constructed of ballast brick. Today, the area hosts a notable collection of prestigious antique galleries.

JAPANTOWN

Stretching for three square blocks along Geary at Fillmore, this multimillion-dollar complex includes a luxury hotel, shops, offices, art galleries, restaurants, theatres, convention facilities and Japanese baths. The complex was designed by one of America's foremost architects, Minoru Yamasaki. The numerous shops offer a wide variety of intriguing wares from Japan and the Orient. On many weekends — particularly during the spring Cherry Blossom Festival — visitors to Japantown can enjoy Japanese music and dancing, tea ceremonies, flower arranging demonstrations, martial arts displays and a variety of other traditional cultural events.

THE MARINA

Colorful Victorian houses along **Union Street** highlight

the Marina, a low-lying district whose grassy pastures earned the name "Cow Hollow" during the last century. A fashionable part of town, the area is making a comeback after the 1989 earthquake. This is old San Francisco preserved and repainted, transformed into clusters of cafes, boutiques and specialty shops. Union Street is as lively by night as by day, with a string of chic restaurants and bars well worth visiting. The grassy **Marina Green**, rimming the bay along Marina Boulevard from the yacht harbor to **Fort Mason**, is a paradise for joggers, kite-flyers, volleyball players and sun-worshippers on warm weekends. Dominating the west end of the Green is the city's favorite classical structure, the majestic **Palace of Fine Arts**. The **St. Francis Yacht Club** is a beehive of activity each April when brightly colored spinnakers and boats of all shapes and sizes dot the bay on opening day of the sailing season.

MISSION DISTRICT

Vibrant, colorful and ethnically diverse, the Mission District is famous for its murals, markets and the landmark the area was named for, **Mission Dolores**. The oldest building in San Francisco, the Spanish mission and its famous cemetery are part of the legacy of the Franciscan padres who played a large role in shaping California's history. On **Mission Street**, established Latin-American restaurants vie with newer Asian eateries, creating a medley of culinary delights ranging from Mexican to Laotian. The heart of the district is at 24th and Mission streets, where you can see striking samples of the area's most prevalent form of artistic expression — the mural. Many more murals, both political and celebratory, brighten the area northeast of this hub on **Balmy Street**. A walk up 24th Street will take you into **Noe Valley**, an off-beat neighborhood filled with bookstores, cafes, boutiques and delis.

NOB HILL

Chic and cosmopolitan, Nob Hill was named after the "nabobs," the rich railroad barons who controlled the rail and shipping trade after the Gold Rush and glorified their successes by building luxurious mansions atop the city's most prominent hill. Now it's the site of the grand hotels: the **Fairmont**, **the Mark Hopkins**, **Stanford Court** and **the Huntington**. **Grace Cathedral** (the imposing Gothic Episcopal church whose design was based in part on Notre Dame of Paris), exclusive clubs, a Masonic temple and sky-high apartment houses crown the summit.

NORTH BEACH

Past headquarters of the "Beat" generation's poets and writers, the coffeehouses of North Beach still provide a haven for conversation, strong espresso and delicious Italian pastries. **Washington Square**, flanked by the spires of **Sts. Peter and Paul Church**, is the center of

TASTE THE WINES FROM CALIFORNIA'S PREMIERE WINE PRODUCING REGION.

Monterey Wine Country

For more information and a free Monterey Wine Country brochure/map & wine tasting guide contact: Monterey Wine Country Associates / 408-375-9400 P.O. Box 1793 / Monterey, California 93942

the Italian community. In this quarter of town, inexpensive restaurants, bakeries and cafes vie for attention with Broadway's neon-lit shows. **Telegraph Hill**, once the site of the city's first semaphore station that signaled approaching vessels, is crowned by **Coit Tower**. The imposing column was erected in 1933 to honor San Francisco's courageous firefighters who saved the city from the devastating fire after the 1906 earthquake. Explore by foot the winding trails that crest the hilltop and continue down the **Filbert Street** steps to encounter the last wooden walkway in the city, tiny **Napier Lane**, tucked among the flowering blossoms of **Grace Marchant Garden**. Nowhere in San Francisco is the feeling of the 1870s better preserved than among these frame cottages. At the bottom of the hill, boldly designed **Levi Plaza** is a handsome addition to the waterfront, with stair-stepped red brick buildings echoing the face of the adjoining hill. Urban offices and restaurants are landscaped to provide walkways, as well as seating around graceful fountains.

PACIFIC HEIGHTS

The most exclusive neighborhood in the city, Pacific Heights overlooks the Marina District, the bay and much of San Francisco. Tiny, perfect gardens, enclosed by high walls, are hidden from passersby. Pacific Heights was settled in the late 19th century by wealthy San Franciscans who competed with Nob Hill aristocracy to build the biggest and best mansions money could buy. Several of these impressive homes are now private schools, consulates or museums. Walking is the best way to view the area's architecture, built on some of the city's steepest hills. **Fillmore Street**, the neighborhood's commercial center, attracts shoppers to its designer boutiques, gourmet food shops, art galleries and gift stores.

PALACE OF FINE ARTS

Reflected in a tranquil lagoon, the Palace of Fine Arts is surrounded by a grassy park where visitors may admire the richly ornamented building. It now houses the **Exploratorium**, a popular hands-on science museum. An integral part of the city's skyline, the Palace of Fine Arts was erected in the Marina District for the Panama-Pacific International Exposition of 1915, which celebrated the completion of the Panama Canal. Not built to last, the domed, colonnaded building became a beloved landmark. By 1967 when the structure began to crumble, funds were raised to restore it — fortifying it in time for the 1989 earthquake.

THE PRESIDIO

Originally established by Spanish conquistadors as their northernmost military post, the Presidio stands today as an impressive 1,440-acre military garrison set in a lush redwood and eucalyptus forest. Used as a training camp during the Civil and Spanish American wars, the Presidio became a refugee camp for the homeless after the 1906 earthquake. In World War I the post became an officers' training camp and then gained importance in World War II as the Western Defense Command Headquarters. Currently the home base for the Sixth U.S. Army, the Presidio is being converted from a military base into parkland. The transfer will be completed in 1994, when the area will be federally preserved as part of the Golden Gate National Recreation Area. Many historic sites at the Presidio are open to the public. An area of fine Victorian houses, known as **Presidio Heights**, is clustered outside the southern perimeter of the army base. **Sacramento Street**, between Spruce and Broderick, features seven blocks of high-fashion boutiques, antique shops and unusual children's shops. **Baker Beach**, off Lincoln Avenue, is a charming cove tucked beneath Mediterranean-style homes along **Seacliff**, a beautiful neighborhood characterized by panoramic views of the Golden Gate.

RUSSIAN HILL

Russian Hill affords some of the best residential views in town. A costly area in which to live, it is also home to the **Art Institute**, established in 1871. Nearby, **Lombard Street** snakes down ten hairpin turns in the space of a single block, descending a 40-degree slope between Hyde and Leavenworth, to earn the title of "World's Crookedest Street." The colorful maze bordered by hydrangeas and other flowers is a perennial must for sightseers. Between Union and Green streets on the hill's eastern slope is carefully protected **Macondray Lane**, a shaded passageway gained by a steep wooden stairway on the Taylor Street side. This charming lane inspired the fictional "Barbary Lane" in Armistead Maupin's serialized *Tales of the City*. Along **Green Street**, notice the elegant octagon house at number 1065, a remnant from the last century. Peaceful **Ina Coolbrith Park** is at Taylor and Vallejo.

SAN FRANCISCO-OAKLAND BAY BRIDGE

The Bay Bridge, built in 1936, is the second-longest suspension bridge in the world (8.4 miles from Oakland to San Francisco). The bridge tunnels through **Yerba Buena Island**, which connects the two sections of the bridge. Once a campground for Indians on fishing expeditions, this hilly island is now a Coast Guard Station. The Bay Bridge cannot be crossed on foot, but you can exit midway at **Treasure Island** for a spectacular view of San Francisco. A low-lying, man-made 400 acres spreading out from the bridge, Treasure Island was created as the site of the 1939 Golden Gate International Exposition. Now a U.S. Naval Base, the island is restricted to the public. Visitors are permitted in the sightseeing area and in the base's museum of nautical memorabilia.

SAN FRANCISCO ZOO

Located at the edge of the Pacific Ocean at Sloat Boulevard, the zoological garden is ranked among the top city zoos in the United States. Special attractions include Penguin Island, where dozens of Magellanic penguins frolic on a specially crafted island in a 200-foot long pool; Gorilla World, a naturalistic exhibit of waterfalls, streams, trees and grass — home to Bwàna and the gorilla family; Prince Charles, a rare white tiger; Pike, the Bay Area's favorite polar bear; the Lion House; Insect Zoo; and Koala Crossing. The latest addition to the zoo is the Primate Discovery Center, exhibiting diverse species of monkeys in lush surroundings, a nocturnal gallery and hands-on educational exhibits. At the Children's Zoo, youngsters are encouraged to feed and pet barnyard animals. Picnic tables, a carousel and a playground add to the activities, and there's plenty of free parking surrounding the zoo.

SOUTH OF MARKET

This evolving area is an eclectic mix of people and lifestyles. With its inexpensive housing and roomy studio lofts, "SOMA" was first popularized by artists and craftsmen. Redevelopment has cleared the flat, run-down blocks South of Market, and long-range plans include new hotels, apartments, shopping and entertainment complexes. **Moscone Center** provides a spacious exhibit floor for conventions, large-scale fairs and computer shows. At **Showplace Square** and the **Gift Center**, you can find designer showrooms of the finest furniture and accessories, and the new **Fashion Center** presents frequent designer shows, some open to the public. Well known for the large and visible gay population of the **Castro District**, South of Market has become increasingly integrated, welcoming art-loving San Franciscans and energetic young people who are transforming the area so dramatically that its restaurants, bars, galleries and clubs now attract patrons from all over the Bay Area.

TWIN PEAKS

Although this Twin Peaks is not the inspiration for David Lynch's television series, it does have its own mystique. Known by Spanish explorers as "Breasts of the Indian Maiden," the 910-foot summit features panoramic views from **Christmas Tree Point**. On a clear night a carpet of twinkling lights covers the city as far as the eye can see. When the fog rolls in, the hillside and homes clinging to it disappear in a shroud of mystery.

UNION SQUARE

Union Square, the lovely park for which the area is named, dates back to the mid-nineteenth century. In 1901 President McKinley broke ground for the square's centerpiece, the bronze "Victory" statue. Union Square

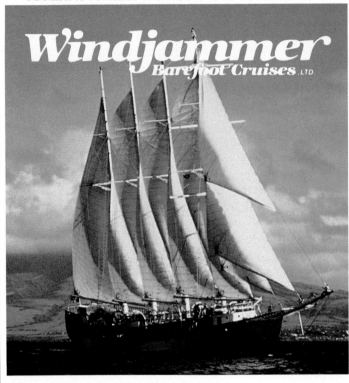

is the heart of the downtown shopping district. Exclusive jewelry and clothing shops include Gucci, Hermes and Tiffany. The square is also the magnet for the city's most elegant department stores.

MUSEUMS

ASIAN ART MUSEUM
Golden Gate Park / 668-8921

Avery Brundage selected San Francisco as the permanent home for his brilliant Asian art collection. The main floor contains Chinese and Korean art objects. Upstairs are the arts of Southeast Asia, Japan, Nepal, Tibet and India. The museum's collection includes the oldest-known dated Chinese image of Buddha (A.D. 338) and the largest collection of Japanese netsuke and inro in the United States.
Open Wednesday through Sunday. Free admission the first Wednesday of every month & Saturdays 10AM to noon

CALIFORNIA ACADEMY OF SCIENCES
Golden Gate Park / 750-7145

The Academy's museum complex offers visitors exhibits from the deepest oceans to the starry skies and all the places in between. The Natural History Museum displays dinosaur models and includes an exhibit that simulates an earthquake. World-renowned Steinhart Aquarium has a large marine life collection, and the Morrison Planetarium features both sky shows and Laserium light shows. Call 750-7138 for recorded information.
Open daily. Free the first Wednesday of every month

CALIFORNIA PALACE OF THE LEGION OF HONOR
Lincoln Park, 34th Ave. at Clement / 863-3330

A copy of the Palais de la Legion d'Honneur in Paris, the museum houses French art treasures, including a Rodin sculpture collection, decorative arts, paintings by Monet, Manet, Degas and Renoir, and a room designed in the period of King Louis XVI. (The museum is closed for the next two years for seismic upgrading.)

EXPLORATORIUM
Palace of Fine Arts / 561-0360

An artfully conceived art and science museum dedicated to discovery, the Exploratorium encourages visitors to see, touch, hear and explore its exhibits.
Open Tuesday through Sunday. Free admission the first Wednesday of every month

HAAS-LILIENTHAL HOUSE
2007 Franklin St. at Jackson / 441-3004

Built in 1886, the Haas-Lilienthal House survived the 1906 earthquake. Period-furnished, it is a stunning example of a Queen Anne Victorian.
Open Wednesday & Sunday

M.H. DE YOUNG MEMORIAL MUSEUM
Golden Gate Park / 863-3330

The city's most diverse art museum includes works of European masters and American artists; pre-Columbian art; traditional arts of Africa, Oceania and the Americas; and classical objects of Egypt, Greece and Rome. Major touring exhibits make a stop here. From May 26 to October 31, 1993, the de Young presents the first-ever exhibit of Teotihuacan art. The pre-Columbian Mexican art is from a civilization that existed 600 years before the Aztecs.
Open Wednesday through Sunday. Free admission daily to children under 12 & to all the first Wednesday & the first Saturday morning of every month

MEXICAN MUSEUM
Fort Mason Center, Building D / 441-0404

Exhibits here are drawn from five areas of art: Pre-Hispanic, Colonial, Folk, Mexican Fine Arts and Mexican-American Fine Arts. The museum shop, La Tienda, offers Mexican arts and crafts.
Open Wednesday through Sunday. Free admission to children under 10 & to all the first Wednesday of every month

MISSION DOLORES
Dolores Ave. at 16th / 621-8203

The oldest building in the city, Mission Dolores was completed by Franciscan fathers in 1791. In the adjacent cemetery you'll find the graves of many famous and infamous early San Franciscans, as well as a grotto memorializing thousands of mission Indians also buried there.
Open daily

MUSEE MECHANIQUE
Cliff House, 1090 Point Lobos Ave. / 386-1170

More than 100 antique mechanical games of skill and chance, including a mechanical 1920s farm and carnival, music boxes, and an old-time penny arcade, make up this privately owned collection of working coin-operated machines.
Open daily. Free admission

MUSEO ITALOAMERICANO
Fort Mason Center, Building C / 673-2200

Dedicated to fostering appreciation of Italian art, architecture and culture, the museum presents a rich and varied collection as well as prestigious traveling exhibitions.
Open Wednesday through Sunday. Free to children under 12

THE MUSEUM OF THE CITY OF SAN FRANCISCO
The Cannery, 2801 Leavenworth St. at Beach / 928-0289

San Francisco's colorful history comes to life at The Museum of the City of San Francisco. The museum's displays of photographs, paintings, art objects, artifacts and maps, including exhibits about the earthquake and fire of 1906 and the Loma Prieta quake of 1989, are fascinating.
Open Wednesday through Sunday. Free admission

THE OLD MINT
88 5th St. at Mission / 744-6830

"The Granite Lady of San Francisco," which first opened in 1874, is one of the finest examples of Federal Classic Revival architecture in the West. The museum features a fascinating collection of U.S. commemorative coins, pioneer gold coins, foreign monies, displays of Western art, antiques, minting equipment and artifacts.
Open Monday through Friday. Free admission

PRESIDIO ARMY MUSEUM
Lincoln Blvd. at Funston in the Presidio / 561-3319

In one of the oldest buildings on the grounds of the Presidio is a display of memorabilia dating from the time it was built in 1776. The exhibits include weapons, uniforms, photographs and military artifacts up to World War I.
Open Tuesday through Sunday. Free admission

SAN FRANCISCO FIRE DEPARTMENT
Pioneer Memorial Museum
655 Presidio Ave. btwn. Bush & Pine / 861-8000

The fire companies of San Francisco, including the historic volunteer units of pre-1866 and the firefighters of today, are celebrated through a remarkable collection of equipment and memorabilia.
Open Thursday through Sunday. Free admission

SAN FRANCISCO MARITIME NATIONAL HISTORIC PARK
Aquatic Park & Hyde St. Pier / 556-3002

Designed to resemble a ship at anchor, this museum features photos, figureheads, harpoons, beautifully crafted ship models and the 19-foot *Mermaid*, sailed by one man from Japan to San Francisco. A short walk takes you to the Hyde Street Pier with its five moored vessels, all afloat and fully restored. Among them is the famous *Balclutha*, one of the last square-rigged vessels to sail around the Horn.
Open daily. Free to seniors & children under 17

SAN FRANCISCO MUSEUM OF MODERN ART
Veterans Memorial Building
Van Ness Ave. at McAllister / 863-8800

Known for its exciting and frequently changing exhibits of contemporary painting, sculpture, video, photography, architecture and design, the museum also has an impressive permanent collection. Devoted to 20th century art, it includes work by Picasso, Matisse and Kandinsky.
Open Tuesday through Sunday. Free admission daily to children 12 & under, and to all the first Tuesday of every month

TOP SPOTS FOR KIDS

BAY AREA DISCOVERY MUSEUM
557 E. Fort Baker, Sausalito / 332-7674

The Bay Area Discovery Museum is a hands-on museum located in a spectacular setting at East Fort Baker, on the north side of the Golden Gate Bridge. The museum's historic buildings house the permanent "San Francisco Bay" and "Building the City" exhibitions and arts studio. Kids will love the fishing boat that rocks, the mock underwater tunnel and the special art and science classes. Don't miss the new Tot Spot for kids under three. This summer the museum will add a children's outdoor sculpture garden and two new exhibit buildings. Some of the shows scheduled will be "The World of Jim Henson: Muppets, Monsters and Magic," a behind-the-scenes look at the muppets, and "What If You Couldn't," to help understand life with disabilities.
Open Tuesday to Sunday in summer; Wednesday to Sunday in winter

CALIFORNIA ACADEMY OF SCIENCES
Golden Gate Park / 750-7145

Laser and sky shows are scheduled regularly at the Morrison Planetarium. The Natural History Museum features lifesize dinosaurs and SafeQuake, a platform that shakes like an earthquake. At the Steinhart Aquarium, kids can watch the staff feed seals, dolphins and penguins.
Open daily

CHILDREN'S DISCOVERY MUSEUM OF SAN JOSE
180 Woz Way at Auzerais St., San Jose / 408-298-5437

Fun interactive exhibits at the largest children's museum in the West. The dramatic purple building is set in a park. Some picnic facilities are available.
Open Tuesday to Sunday

CHILDREN'S FAIRYLAND
Lakeside Park at Lake Merritt, Oakland / 510-452-2259

Appealing mostly to younger children, Fairyland's outdoor setting features themes from nursery rhymes and fairytales, with rides, animals, play areas, puppet shows and special events.
Open daily in summer; Wednesday to Sunday in spring & fall; weekends only in winter

EXPLORATORIUM
Palace of Fine Arts / 561-0360

Hours of fascinating science exhibits. The hands-on museum offers special events throughout the year. To arrange tickets for the Tactile Dome, a sensory exhibit where visitors crawl through a dark tunnel, call several weeks in advance at 561-0362. (The Tactile Dome is not recommended for children under seven.)
Open Tuesday to Sunday

GOLDEN GATE PARK CHILDREN'S PLAYGROUND
Bowling Green Dr. at Kennedy / 666-7107

At the eastern end of the park, the playground has slides, tire swings and lots of jungle gyms to climb on.

OK, so we couldn't agree on what to do on our family vacation.

I dreamed of going on a cruise. Anthony

WHITEWATER FALLS

begged to go flying. And Vanessa had her heart

TOP GUN

set on going stargazing.

Finally, Mike said, "Why not do it all?"

STAR TREK

Paramount's

GREAT AMERICA®

Where The Magic Of The Movies Meets The Thrills Of A Lifetime.

Hwy. 101 at Great America Pkwy. in Santa Clara. (408) 988-1776   TM & Copyright© 1993 A Paramount Communications Company. All Rights Reserved.

Kids can ride on an antique carousel nearby.
Open daily; carousel open Thursday to Sunday

LAWRENCE HALL OF SCIENCE
Centennial Dr. near Grizzly Peak Blvd.
Berkeley / 510-642-5132

Hands-on science museum with a variety of biology and physics labs. The museum also features exhibits on lasers, earthquakes and other topics, planetarium shows and special events throughout the year.
Open daily

MARINE WORLD/AFRICA USA
Marine World Pkwy., off Hwy. 80
Vallejo / 707-643-6722

If you would like to take a ferry to the park, contact the Red & White Fleet at 546-2896, leaving from Pier 41 at Fisherman's Wharf. Marine World offers great marine animal shows, tigers and elephants, chimps and parrots, and lots of animals to see up close. Kids can ride elephants and watch whales and dolphins perform. The newest attractions are an underwater tunnel where you can see sharks swim around and above you and "Dinosaurs," a prehistoric adventure, open April to October. The waterskiing shows are spectacular, and the special playground provides hours of fun.
Open daily in summer; Wednesday to Sunday in winter

MONTEREY BAY AQUARIUM
Southern end of Cannery Row
Monterey / 408-648-4888

The aquarium is one of the largest in the country. A favorite destination for the entire family, the aquarium presents several types of marine habitats. At the Tide Pool, kids can touch starfish, sea anemones and other marine life. They can also pet bat rays gliding in a special pool, see fish being fed by a skindiver in the kelp forest and watch otters play.
Open daily

PARAMOUNT'S GREAT AMERICA
Great America Pkwy. exit off Hwy. 101
Santa Clara / 408-988-1776

Thrills for all ages at Northern California's largest theme park. Shows, games and roller coaster rides such as the Grizzly, the Demon and the Vortex, the only stand-up roller coaster west of the Mississippi. The park's 34 rides include a free-fall and a ride down whitewater falls. Its newest ride, Top Gun, is a mind-boggling inverted steel coaster named after the movie. Since the park was acquired by Paramount Pictures, many of its attractions and theatrical shows are now based on the company's movie and television characters.
Open daily in summer; weekends only in spring and fall; closed mid-October to mid-March. Call for operating hours

PIER 39
Embarcadero & Beach St. / 981-PIER

Voted by San Francisco schoolchildren as their favorite place to go in the city, Pier 39 has a carousel, video arcade and lots of specialty shops. Jugglers and street artists perform daily. On the waterfront, sea lions make themselves at home at Pier 39's K-dock.
Open daily

RAGING WATERS
2333 S. White Rd. at Tully, San Jose / 408-238-9900

Splash into more than thirty pools via twisting, slippery slides at this water amusement park. Older kids like the inner-tube ride and the breathtaking speed slides. For younger children, there are wading pools and gentler slides. Food and picnic areas are available.
Open daily in summer; weekends only in September

THE RANDALL MUSEUM
199 Museum Way off Roosevelt / 554-9600

Dedicated to arousing children's interest in the world around them, this museum's animal room houses a fascinating variety of live animals and includes a petting area. Craft and nature classes are also offered.
Open Tuesday to Saturday

ROARING CAMP
Graham Hill Rd., Felton / 408-335-4484

Six miles north of Santa Cruz, Roaring Camp was a loggers' camp in 1880. Today, it's the starting point for an exciting ride up Bear Mountain aboard an authentic steam logging train. The 75-minute ride goes through a beautiful redwood grove. Special events are planned at the park through the summer, including old-time entertainment and chuckwagon barbecues. On Memorial Day, men dressed as Union and Confederate soldiers reenact battles from the Civil War. The event is the largest such commemoration in the West.
Open daily in summer; Wednesday to Sunday in winter

SAN FRANCISCO ZOO
45th Ave. & Sloat Blvd. / 753-7061

The zoo has more than 300 species of animals. Call for the feeding times for the penguins and big cats and for the schedule of shows at Insect Zoo. At Children's Zoo, kids can feed and pet farm animals, see baby birds hatch and watch prairie dogs pop out of their burrows. The zoo also has a carousel, playground and several picnic areas for family fun.
Open daily

SANTA CRUZ BEACH BOARDWALK
400 Beach St. at Cliff, Santa Cruz / 408-423-5590

A crowded, corny, totally American boardwalk by the beach, with 27 different rides, including a ferris wheel, two roller coasters, a merry-go-round and bumper cars.

DO THE WILD THING

MARINE WORLD AFRICA USA

Come Closer to the wild things at the only park of its kind in the world – Marine World Africa USA.

Witness the true magnificence of the killer whale. Watch Bengal tigers romp and play with their trainers. Walk through a tropical rainforest filled with butterflies. Experience what it's like to feed a giraffe. Match your strength playing tug-o-war with a five ton elephant. And now, enter through a crystal clear tunnel to our awe-inspiring undersea world of tropical sharks at the all-new **Shark Experience!**

Don't miss the Bay Area's premiere family attraction!

Open daily in the summer, Wed.-Sun. in the fall, winter & spring. For more information, call (707) 643-ORCA. Marine World Africa USA, in Vallejo, is located 30 miles northeast of San Francisco. From I-80, take the Marine World Pkwy (Hwy 37) exit.

Red & White Fleet offers ferry service to Marine World from San Francisco's Fisherman's Wharf, Pier 41. Call (415) 546-2700 for more information, Transportation and tickets also available from Gray Line. Call (415) 558-9400.

Marine World Parkway, Vallejo, CA 94589
Marine World Foundation • a nonprofit organization

There is also an indoor arcade with miniature golf and video games. Kids love it.
Open daily in summer; weekends only the rest of the year

TILDEN REGIONAL PARK
2501 Grizzly Peak, off Canon Dr.
Berkeley / 510-635-0135

Beautiful Tilden Park offers more than just trail and picnic areas. There's a lake for swimming, an old carousel, a miniature steam train, a Little Farm, pony rides and a botanical garden.
Open daily

WINCHESTER MYSTERY HOUSE
525 S. Winchester Blvd. at Olsen
San Jose / 408-247-2101

The house was built by an heiress to the Winchester rifle fortune to appease occult spirits. She believed she would die if construction on her house ever stopped. Sarah Winchester kept carpenters working around the clock for 38 years until her death. The result: a bizarre but marvelous mansion with 160 rooms, thousands of windows, switchback stairways that lead nowhere and symbols scattered throughout to shoo away ghosts.
Open daily

CHILDREN'S ENTERTAINMENT

KIDSHOWS
655 Thirteenth St., Preservation Park
Oakland / 510-527-4977

Kidshows's presentations, which include performances by the Berkeley Ballet, musicians, folk dancers, storytellers, magicians and puppeteers, are offered at various Bay Area locations.

MAKE-A-CIRCUS
Fort Mason, Building C / 776-8477

Make-A-Circus presents free festival days in Bay Area parks during the summer, combining a musical circus/theatre performance, a circus skills workshop and a grand finale during which the audience presents its new skills.

PICKLE FAMILY CIRCUS
400 Missouri St. / 826-0747

The Pickle Family Circus tours the nation each year, returning to the Bay Area to present its annual holiday show at the Palace of Fine Arts. Order tickets well in advance. The group occasionally presents shows at other times of the year.

SAN FRANCISCO YOUNG PERFORMERS THEATRE
Fort Mason, Building C / 346-5550

Offering a delightful program, the Young Performers Theatre features shows performed by children and professionals, birthday parties and classes.

SPECTATOR SPORTS

BASEBALL
OAKLAND A'S
Oakland Coliseum / 510-638-0500

April to October. For tickets, call 510-762-BASS.

SAN FRANCISCO GIANTS
Candlestick Park / 467-8000

April to October. For tickets, call 982-9400. Tickets may also be purchased by phone from BASS at 510-762-BASS or in person at Giants Dugout, 170 Grant Ave.

BASKETBALL
GOLDEN STATE WARRIORS
Oakland Coliseum Arena / 510-638-6300

November to April. For tickets, call 510-762-BASS.

FOOTBALL
SAN FRANCISCO 49ERS
Candlestick Park / 468-2249

August to December.

ICE HOCKEY
SAN JOSE SHARKS
Cow Palace / 408-28-SHARK

October to April. For tickets, call 510-762-BASS. In August 1993, the Sharks move into their permanent home, the San Jose Arena.

YACHTING
ST. FRANCIS YACHT CLUB
Marina Blvd. & Baker St. / 563-6363

San Francisco's sailing season officially opens in late April with regatta races and special events on the bay. The St. Francis Yacht Club also has information on other races throughout the year.

SPORTS ACTIVITIES

GOLF
GLENEAGLES GOLF COURSE
McLaren Park, 2100 Sunnydale Ave. / 587-2425

Nine-hole course.

GOLDEN GATE PARK GOLF COURSE
Golden Gate Park, off 47th Ave. & Fulton / 751-8987

Nine-hole course.

HARDING PARK GOLF COURSE
Harding Rd. & Skyline Blvd. / 664-4690

Eighteen-hole and nine-hole course at Lake Merced.

EXPLORATORIUM

The Museum of Science, Art and Human Perception

There are two models for great
American amusement centers…Disneyland and
the Exploratorium. This place feeds all the senses."

Tuesday through Sunday, 10am-5pm, and Wednesday until 9:30pm
3601 Lyon Street (inside the Palace of Fine Arts), San Francisco, CA (415)561-0360

FORT MASON CENTER

• A KALEIDOSCOPE OF THE ARTS •

• SF African American Historical & Cultural Society •

• The Mexican Museum • Museo ItaloAmericano •

• Bayfront Gallery • SF Craft & Folk Art Museum •

• SF Museum of Modern Art Rental Gallery •

• National Liberty Ship Memorial SS Jeremiah O'Brien •

• Greens Restaurant • Cowell Theater • Herbst & Festival Pavilions •

• Life On The Water • Magic Theatre • Young Performers Theatre •

• Fort Mason Art Center • SF Children's Art Center •

• Special Events • Conferences • Workshops • Classes •

Buchanan Street at Marina Boulevard, San Francisco
• free parking • spectacular views • easy MUNI access •

24-hour recorded message of events: 415 441 5705
Information & Calendar of Events: 415 441 5706

LINCOLN MUNICIPAL GOLF COURSE
34th Ave. & Clement / 221-9911

Eighteen-hole course.

SWIMMING
INTERNATIONAL CENTER
50 Oak St. at Franklin / 863-7676

The pool is part of the low-cost International Center health club owned by the Catholic archdiocese. For a small monthly fee you may also use the weight room, basketball and volleyball courts, and sauna.

JEWISH COMMUNITY CENTER
3200 California St. at Presidio / 346-6040

This is a membership club, but you can enroll for swim or exercise classes in their large pool without being a member. They also offer one-day passes. Other facilities include courts for basketball, racquetball, handball, volleyball and squash; Nautilus, exercycles, rowing machines, Universal machine, sauna, jacuzzi and aerobic classes.

SAN FRANCISCO RECREATION & PARKS
Aquatics Division / 753-7026

The city's public swimming pools have a full program of lessons, pool exercise and lap swims.

YMCA
220 Golden Gate at Leavenworth / 885-0460
169 Steuart St. at Mission / 957-9622
333 Eucalyptus St. at 21st Ave. / 759-9622

All three of these Ys are coed and have good-sized lap pools in addition to their other facilities — from weight rooms, Nautilus equipment and saunas to a full program of fitness classes.

TENNIS
GOLDEN GATE PARK TENNIS
Kennedy Dr. near 3rd Ave. / 753-7001

Twenty-one courts surrounded by trees are on a first-come, first-served basis on weekdays, but usually there's no wait. Reservations are required on weekends. A full-time pro and both private and group lessons for adults and children are available.

SAN FRANCISCO RECREATION & PARKS
Tennis Division / 753-7032

There are 132 free tennis courts in San Francisco in addition to the Golden Gate Park courts. Call for a free map and for a brochure listing classes, courts and a calendar of tennis events.

ATTRACTIONS

CALENDAR OF EVENTS

For specific dates, call the San Francisco Convention & Visitors Bureau at 391-2000.

JANUARY

SAN FRANCISCO SYMPHONY
Opening of the San Francisco Symphony's season. Performances run through June, Davies Symphony Hall.

FEBRUARY

CHINESE NEW YEAR CELEBRATION
Week of festivities to mark the Chinese New Year. Events in Chinatown include a parade with floats, gongs, firecrackers, snake and stick dragons.

CHILDREN'S KITE FESTIVAL
Kite-flying and kite-making demonstrations, Pier 39.

SAN FRANCISCO BALLET
The ballet opens its season. Performances run through May, War Memorial Opera House.

MARCH

TULIPMANIA
Pier 39 puts 15,000 tulips on display. Guided tours, gardening seminars and other events.

ST. PATRICK'S DAY CELEBRATION
Irish dancers, marching bands and pipers parade up Market Street in honor of St. Patrick's Day.

MACY'S EASTER FLOWER SHOW
Easter flowers, both native and exotic, on display at Macy's downtown store.

APRIL

FESTIVAL OF ANIMATION
Animated short films at the Palace of Fine Arts Theatre.

UNION STREET EASTER PARADE
Parade and Easter hat contest on Union Street.

CHERRY BLOSSOM FESTIVAL
The cherry blossoms are in bloom at the Japanese Tea Garden in Golden Gate Park. In Japantown, their arrival is celebrated with a parade, taiko drum concerts, martial arts displays and bonsai and ikebana demonstrations.

INTERNATIONAL STREET PERFORMERS FESTIVAL
Jugglers, mimes and other street artists perform at Pier 39.

SAN FRANCISCO LANDSCAPE GARDEN SHOW
Largest indoor garden show in the West. Lectures, demonstrations and showcase gardens, Fort Mason.

SAN FRANCISCO INTERNATIONAL FILM FESTIVAL
Festival presents American and European films. Parties and special events feature stars and celebrity filmmakers, AMC Kabuki 8 Cinemas.

MAY

BAY TO BREAKERS
San Francisco's legendary race from the bay to the Pacific. Third Sunday in May, with more than 80,000 runners and as many spectators.

CINCO DE MAYO
Mexico's Independence Day. Grand parade in the Mission District with salsa, samba and mariachi bands.

CARNAVAL
Celebration and parade in the Mission District. Brazilian and Caribbean samba, belly dancers and West Indian steel bands.

UNION STREET SPRING FESTIVAL
Arts and crafts booths, entertainers and gourmet wine and food fair on Union Street.

JUNE

ETHNIC DANCE FESTIVAL
Folk ensembles from around the world perform at the Palace of Fine Arts Theatre.

CABLE CAR BELL RINGING COMPETITION
Cable car grip conductors and amateurs compete for the title of champion bell ringer, Union Square.

FESTIVAL OF THE VIEWING OF THE MOON
Three-day festival in honor of the moon. Traditional Japanese food, arts and crafts and music in Japantown.

HAIGHT-ASHBURY STREET FAIR
Popular festival on Haight Street. Food and crafts booths, street performers, music bands from reggae to heavy metal.

NORTH BEACH FAIR
North Beach festival celebrates the neighborhood's Italian heritage with arts, crafts, music and Italian food served at outdoor cafes.

STERN GROVE MIDSUMMER MUSIC FESTIVAL
Free Sunday afternoon performances at Stern Grove. The summer festival includes performances by the San Francisco Symphony and Bay Area artists.

GAY FREEDOM DAY CELEBRATION
Largest gay pride celebration in the world. Morning parade, followed by music and entertainment at the Civic Center.

JULY

JAZZ & ALL THAT ART ON FILLMORE
Outdoors jazz fair on Fillmore Street. Arts and crafts, gourmet food booths.

FOURTH OF JULY CELEBRATION
Music and entertainment at Crissy Field on the waterfront. Fifty-gun salute followed by fireworks.

MIDSUMMER MOZART FESTIVAL
All-Mozart program through August, Herbst Theatre.

SAN FRANCISCO SYMPHONY POPS FESTIVAL
Summer Pops concert series runs through August, Civic Auditorium.

SUMMER FESTIVAL OF PERFORMING ARTS
Free weekend performances through September at the Music Concourse, Golden Gate Park.

SAN FRANCISCO MIME TROUPE
Political theatre, music and dance. The mime troupe gives free performances in Bay Area parks throughout the summer.

COMEDY CELEBRATION DAY
Bay Area comedians in a free performance at Golden Gate Park.

AUGUST

SAN FRANCISCO SHAKESPEARE FESTIVAL
Free Shakespeare performances, Golden Gate Park.

NIHONMACHI STREET FAIR
Street fair in Japantown. Arts and crafts, food and children's events.

PACIFIC STATES CRAFT FAIR
Juried craft fair in all media from paper to glass, Fort Mason.

SAN FRANCISCO FAIR FLOWER SHOW
Largest juried flower show in the West, San Francisco County Fair Building, Golden Gate Park.

SEPTEMBER

A LA CARTE, A LA PARK
Gourmet food festival, Golden Gate Park.

SAN FRANCISCO OPERA
The opera season runs from September to December, War Memorial Opera House.

FESTIVAL DE LAS AMERICAS
Latin American food and arts festival, Mission District.

BAY AREA ROBOT OLYMPICS
Amateur robot builders compete and display their robots, The Exploratorium.

LEAP SANDCASTLE-BUILDING CONTEST
Sandcastle-building contest for architects, Aquatic Park.

SAN FRANCISCO BLUES FESTIVAL
Blues performances at Fort Mason and at the Justin Hermann Plaza downtown.

OCTOBER

COUNTRY IN THE CITY FESTIVAL
Two-day festival of new country music groups, Golden Gate Park.

CASTRO STREET FAIR
Food booths, crafts, entertainment on Castro Street.

FESTA ITALIANA
Italian street festival at Fisherman's Wharf. Italian entertainers, bocce ball tournaments, dancing and cooking demonstrations.

COLUMBUS DAY CELEBRATION
Week of commemorative events in downtown San Francisco, culminating with a parade through North Beach.

FLEET WEEK
Parade of ships under the Golden Gate Bridge and flying maneuvers performed by the Navy's crack aviation team, the Blue Angels.

GREAT HALLOWEEN & PUMPKIN FESTIVAL
Trick-or-treating, children's parade, hay rides, pumpkin festival and pumpkin-carving contests, Clement Street.

SAN FRANCISCO JAZZ FESTIVAL
National jazz artists perform at venues in San Francisco.

NOVEMBER

INTERNATIONAL WINE TASTING FESTIVAL
Largest public wine tasting in California, San Francisco County Fair Building, Golden Gate Park.

ENCUENTRO DEL CANTO POPULAR
Latin American folk music, Palace of Fine Arts Theatre.

SAN FRANCISCO HARVEST FESTIVAL
Country-fair festival at the Civic Center. Folk dancers, bluegrass, country bands, crafts and country cooking.

DICKENS CHRISTMAS FAIR
Holiday fair with a cast of characters from the "Christmas Carol," Fisherman's Wharf.

TRADITIONAL TREE LIGHTING CEREMONY
Tree lighting at Pier 39 on Thanksgiving Eve. Caroling, an appearance by Santa and favorite Disney characters.

DECEMBER

A CHRISTMAS CAROL
Dickens's classic performed by the American Conservatory Theatre repertory, Orpheum Theatre.

THE NUTCRACKER
The San Francisco Ballet's traditional holiday performance, War Memorial Opera House.

THE MESSIAH
Handel's masterpiece presented by the San Francisco Symphony Orchestra, Davies Symphony Hall.

HOLIDAY CELEBRATIONS
Pier 39, Ghirardelli Square, Crocker Galleria, the Embarcadero Center and San Francisco's major department stores plan special events throughout the holiday season.

and stores. As diverse as the city's residents, they offer something for every taste — from the elegant boutiques of Sacramento Street to the funky shops of Haight Street, where some trends are born and others refuse to die.

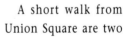

Somewhere between the extremes is the casual California look, which started with Levi's jeans and gradually conquered the world. Other local companies, including Esprit, Banana Republic and the now ubiquitous Gap, helped set the standard for modern relaxed dressing.

Today, San Francisco style can be anything from designer gowns to baggy pants and a ribbed T-shirt. The easiest place to shop remains Union Square, recognized worldwide as San Francisco's best shopping address. On the square itself are no less than four department stores: Neiman Marcus, Macy's, Saks Fifth Avenue and the city's own I. Magnin. Within a few blocks of the square are such prestigious names as Hermes, Chanel, Gianni Versace, Bottega Veneta, Escada, Emporio Armani and Tiffany.

Introduced by David Becker

A short walk from Union Square are two multilevel complexes: the San Francisco Shopping Centre, home to Nordstrom, the city's newest department store, and the Crocker Galleria. Both centers offer a unique mix of specialty stores and restaurants, with a distinctly urban ambiance that sets them apart from their suburban cousins.

Whether you're looking for a specific item or just looking, save time enough to browse. From Chinatown to Fisherman's Wharf, from Ghirardelli Square to the Embarcadero, San Francisco will delight you with the range and originality of its shops and merchandise.

David Becker is president of Jay David, Inc., which owns and operates San Francisco's Gianni Versace stores, Diagonale on Sutter Street and Versus Gianni Versace in the Crocker Galleria.

Thank you: Laise Adzer; Joey Chase, Mitzi Land, EPIC Models

SHOPPING DIRECTORY

SHOPPING AREAS

THE CANNERY
2801 Leavenworth St. at Beach & Jefferson
Fisherman's Wharf

Formerly the world's largest fruit canning plant, The Cannery was converted in 1967 into a shopping center, modeled after European marketplaces. The two-building, three-level brick structure incorporates winding walkways, arches, bridges and balconies, with a flower-filled courtyard playing host to various street performers. You'll find terrific sweaters at **Toppers**, esoteric gift items at **Aerial**, and specialty food items at **The Cannery Gourmet Market**. If you're here at night you can catch a show at **Cobb's Comedy Club** or dine at **Ale Garden Cafe** or **Cafe Rigatoni**. A supper club, **Quiet Storm**, offers a spectacular bay view and features jazz several nights a week.

CROCKER GALLERIA
50 Post St. btwn. Post & Sutter at Kearny
Downtown

Located near Union Square, Crocker Galleria contains 50 shops, restaurants and services under a spectacular glass dome. Modeled after Milan's vast Galleria Vittorio Emmanuelle, the three-level pavilion features exciting fashion designs from **Gianni Versace**, **Nicole Miller** and **Mondi**. You'll enjoy shopping at **Polo/Ralph Lauren**, **Marimekko** and **The Limited** and dining at restaurants including **Circolo**, **SRO** and **Tortola**.
Open Monday through Friday 9:30AM to 6PM; Saturday 10AM to 5PM; closed Sunday. Underground parking available at the Sutter Street entrance

EMBARCADERO CENTER
Clay & Sacramento btwn. Battery & Drumm
Financial District

Eight blocks of shops, restaurants, galleries and services comprise the Embarcadero Center, anchored on either end by the **Hyatt Regency** and **Park Hyatt** hotels. Set on three levels of open-air plazas interconnected by pedestrian walkways, the center offers shoppers sunny places to relax amid landscaped grounds and large sculptures. Shopping for gifts is easy at shops such as **The Nature Company**, **Williams-Sonoma** and **Game Gallery**. Try **AnnTaylor**, **Georgiou**, **Banana Republic** or **The Limited** for women's apparel; **Alta Moda**, **Structure**, **The Gap** or **Hastings** for menswear; and **Cinnabon**, **Oh-La-La!** or **Los Chiles** for a quick bite. If you have time for more leisurely dining, there's **Harbor Village**, **Chevy's**, **Splendido's**, **Park Grill** and a host of other fine restaurants.

FILLMORE STREET
btwn. Jackson & Sutter, Pacific Heights

The premier shopping area in Pacific Heights, Fillmore

Street has an air of quiet sophistication. Here, you'll discover boutiques carrying the latest in designer fashions, vintage clothing shops, gift shops, galleries, sidewalk cafes and outstanding restaurants. Stop by **Spinelli's** for a cup of cafe au lait before visiting shops like **Jim-Elle**, **Toujours**, **Coup de Chapeau** and **Avant Premiere**. For dinner, try **Oritalia** or the **Elite Cafe**.

GHIRARDELLI SQUARE
900 North Point at Polk & Larkin
Fisherman's Wharf

One of San Francisco's best-known landmarks, Ghirardelli Square was a working chocolate factory from 1900 to 1967. Today, its brick buildings house distinctive shops and restaurants. For women's fashions, there's **Ann Taylor** and **Operetta**, while **Benetton** carries well-made casuals for men and women. Notable gift shops include **Goosebumps** and **The Sharper Image**. Some of the city's most celebrated restaurants, many with sweeping bay views, are here: **Gaylord India**, **The Mandarin** and **McCormick & Kuleto's Seafood Restaurant**.

JAPAN CENTER
Post St. btwn. Laguna & Fillmore, Western Addition

Designed by premier American architect Minoru Yamasaki, the Japan Center opened in 1968. The outdoor complex, landscaped with flowering plum and cherry trees, fountains and a river of stones, stretches for three square blocks. Home to the annual spring Cherry Blossom Festival, the Japan Center contains numerous shops carrying fine imported wares from Asia, as well as restaurants, sushi bars, hotels, a theatre complex and Japanese-style baths.

PIER 39
Waterfront at Embarcadero & Beach
Fisherman's Wharf

Once an abandoned cargo pier, Pier 39 opened as a festival marketplace in 1978. Now the third most visited attraction in the country, the pier houses two levels of one-of-a-kind shops, restaurants and entertaining diversions. Pier 39's specialty shops carry items as diverse as puppets, kites, teddy bears, Christmas decorations, baseball caps and hammocks. Restaurants include **Yet Wah**, **Old Swiss House** and the historic **Eagle Cafe**, a San Francisco landmark frequented by fishermen, dock workers and longshoremen since the turn of the century. A handcrafted carousel, an arcade, street performers and lots of snack and food stands make this a wonderful place to shop with children.

SACRAMENTO STREET
btwn. Locust & Baker, Presidio Heights

Located in charming Presidio Heights, Sacramento Street is one of San Francisco's more delightful shopping areas. A stroll along the seven blocks between Spruce and Broderick streets uncovers an exciting array of upscale, high fashion shops such as **Susan's**, **Max Nugus Fashions** and **Justine**. Objets d'art and antiques at **Les Poisson**, **Santa Fe**, **Maxine's** and **Sue Fisher King**, and unique children's stores — including **Dottie Doolittle** and **Kindersport** — are also among Sacramento Street's many temptations. If all that shopping works up an appetite, **Tortola's** Southwestern cuisine or the quiet courtyard settings of **Tuba Garden** and **The Magic Flute** are nearby antidotes.

SAN FRANCISCO SHOPPING CENTRE
865 Market St. at 5th, Downtown / 495-5656

Six spiral escalators — the only ones in the United States — carry shoppers through a central, oval-shaped atrium marked by lavish use of bronze and Italian marble, and topped by a retractable skylight. Five upper floors are occupied by **Nordstrom**, while more than 90 specialty shops, including **Adrienne Vittadini**, **J. Crew**, **Matsuzakaya**, **Kenneth Cole**, **P. Keller**, **Mondi** and **Vasari**, fill out the lower floors. San Francisco Shopping Centre is serviced by cable car, bus, Muni Metro and BART, but if you must drive, valet parking is available.

STONESTOWN GALLERIA
19th Ave. at Winston, Sunset District

Completely remodeled from a low-key shopping center into an elegant two-story mall with a soaring atrium, marble floors and a grand piano player, Stonestown Galleria has shopping finds for the whole family. **Nordstrom** and **Emporium**, the mall's two department stores, are at either end, with loads of great shopping in between. There's **Williams-Sonoma** and **Pottery Barn** for housewares, **9 West** for shoes, **The Gap** and **Cignal** for casual wear, **Papyrus** for cards and stationery, **Yountville**, **Gap Kids** and **Gymboree** for kids, and lots more. A food gallery in the center of the mall offers everything from pizza to steak.

UNION SQUARE
btwn. Post, Stockton, Geary & Powell, Downtown

San Francisco's premier shopping area, Union Square is the most prestigious address in town. This is where you'll find the most fashionable names in retail: **Arthur Beren**, **Bally**, **Cartier**, **Gucci**, **Hermes**, **Gump's**, **MaxMara**, **Tiffany**, **Shreve & Co.**, **Sulka**, **Louis Vuitton**, **Gianni Versace** and **Escada**. The big department stores are represented by **Macy's**, **I. Magnin**, **Neiman Marcus** and **Saks Fifth Avenue**. At the west end of Union Square is the **Westin St. Francis Hotel**, a majestic symbol of old San Francisco grandeur; at the east is the two-block-long Maiden Lane, a peaceful, tree-lined walk filled with exclusive boutiques and galleries.

Come See Why America's #1 Place To Save On Coats Is Becoming America's #1 Place To Save On Everything Your Family Wants To Wear

Save 25%-60% and even more* *every day* on the latest famous label women's dresses, suits, sportswear and accessories, men's suits, furnishings and sportswear, top name clothes for kids of all ages, luxury linens, baby furniture and, of course, more coats, raincoats, jackets and leathers than *anyone!* You get the best for a lot less at Burlington Coat Factory.

Burlington Coat Factory

Not affiliated with
Burlington Industries

Five Bay Area Locations
San Francisco Downtown at 5th & Howard (415) 495-7234
Hayward La Playa Drive (opp. Southland Mall) (510) 782-7073
Daly City Lake Merced Blvd. & Southgate Ave. (415) 997-0733
Pittsburg Century Plaza Shopping Center (510) 754-5513
San Jose West Gate Mall (408) 378-COAT
OPEN EVERY DAY INCLUDING SUNDAY

*Off normal retail prices elsewhere.   *Major Credit Cards Accepted*

UNION STREET
btwn. Steiner & Gough, Marina District

The heart of San Francisco's historic Cow Hollow area, Union Street is lined with beautifully preserved Victorian and Edwardian houses, now home to seven blocks of charming shops, galleries, cafes, restaurants and bed-and-breakfast inns. Discover **Bebe** and **Laura Ashley** for women's clothing, **Sy Aal** for menswear, **Familiar** for children's apparel and **Kenneth Cole** for high fashion footwear. Enhance your living environment at antique stores like **Fumiki**. Other stores of note include **Oggetti**, purveyors of Florentine hand-marbleized papers and **Charlotte's Web**, carrying books and gifts for children. Scores of cafes, gourmet takeout stores, restaurants and bars await when it's time to refresh yourself.

BAY AREA SHOPPING CENTERS

JACK LONDON SQUARE
Broadway & Embarcadero, Oakland Waterfront
510-814-6000

At the water's edge, Jack London Square is a special spot to shop, dine and daydream. You can reach the square by car or by ferry from San Francisco, leaving from either Pier 39 or the Ferry Building. Shoppers will find one-of-a-kind items from around the world at **Cost Plus** and **Pier 1 Imports**, as well as great retail values at **Barnes & Noble Bookstore** and **Sneaker's Plus**. There are many restaurants to choose from, including **Scott's**, **Jack's**, **Il Pescatore**, **El Torito**, **Kincaid's** and **Old Spaghetti Factory**. On Sundays, Jack London Square sponsors a popular Farmer's Market.
Store hours vary; most shops open daily. Metered on-street and garage parking

POWELL STREET PLAZA
Christie Ave., Emeryville

Just minutes from the San Francisco Bay Bridge, Powell Street Plaza has a highly visible and easily accessible location at the Powell Street Plaza Exit off Interstate 80. The Emeryville shopping center has 24 stores with a variety of selections. Major apparel stores include **Ross Dress for Less**, **Clothestime**, **Shoe Pavilion**, **Men's Wearhouse** and **Such a Business** for children's furnishings. You can get everything from books to electronics at the center's specialty shops: **Crown Books**, **Headlines**, **Tower Records**, **Copeland's Sports** and **Circuit City**. For a quick bite, there's **Bettore's Pizza**, **Sundaes Yogurt Plus** and **Hobee's Restaurant**.
Open Monday through Saturday 10AM to 6PM, Sunday noon to 5PM. Free parking

280 METRO CENTER
Colma & Junipero Serra Blvd., Colma

Fifteen minutes from downtown San Francisco, 280 Metro Center has the greatest selection of promotional retailers in the area. Located off Interstate 280 at Colma and Junipero Serra boulevards, the shopping center's 35 stores offer quality products at outstanding values. For apparel and shoes, try **Marshalls**, **Shoe Depot**, **Shoe Works**, **Nordstrom Rack** and **Kids'R Us**. For home furnishings, **New York Fabrics**, **Pier 1 Imports**, **Home Depot** and **Welcome Home** are among the many outlets featured. Sports equipment is available at **Herman's Sporting Goods** and **FILA Factory Outlet**. You can get jewelry at **The Diamond Center**, and you will find a variety of items at **Crown Books**, **Paper Image**, **Beauty Store & More**, **Videots** and **39 Minute Photo**. Family entertainment includes the **Discovery Zone**, a children's creative play center, the **UA-6** theatres and casual dining at **Jil's Cafe** and **Who's Pizza**.
Open Monday through Friday 10AM to 9PM, Saturday 10AM to 6PM, Sunday noon to 6PM. Free parking

THE VILLAGE AT CORTE MADERA
1554 Redwood Hwy. at Paradise Dr. & Hwy. 101
Corte Madera / 924-8557

Located in scenic Southern Marin, The Village at Corte Madera is a truly unique shopping experience. The beautifully designed open-air center is distinguished as much by its lush landscaping and contemporary architecture as by its distinctive collection of stores, including more than 90 shops. **Nordstrom**, **Macy's**, **Ann Taylor**, **Eddie Bauer**, **Gap**, **Nature Company**, **Crate & Barrel** and many other specialty stores provide the best in fashions, home interiors, gifts and specialty items. The selection of restaurants and cafes offers a bounty of international cuisines for a quick bite or for more leisurely dining. At The Village at Corte Madera, shopping is as relaxed and inviting as Marin itself.
Open Monday through Friday 10AM to 9PM, Saturday 10AM to 6PM, Sunday noon to 6PM. Free parking

DEPARTMENT STORES

BURLINGTON COAT FACTORY
899 Howard St. at Fifth / 495-7234

Famous as America's number one place to save on coats, Burlington Coat Factory is also America's number one place to save on everything your family needs to wear. You'll find incomparable values in women's designer label sportswear and dresses, men's suits, sportswear and furnishings, clothing for children of all ages, plus linens and bath accessories. Burlington Coat Factory also carries an average of 15,000 coats for men, women and children in each of its Bay Area stores. Everything is offered at savings of 25 to 60 percent every day. In addition to its downtown San Francisco location, there are stores in Hayward, Daly City, Pittsburg and San Jose.

SHOPPING

EMPORIUM
835 Market St. at 5th / 764-2222
Stonestown Galleria / 753-4000

You can outfit your whole family as well as redecorate your home at this full-line department store. Branches can be found throughout Northern California, but the downtown store is the "soul" of the company where generations of San Franciscans have shopped.

I. MAGNIN
Union Square / 362-2100

One of San Francisco's oldest businesses, I. Magnin was founded in 1876 and since then has continued its successful merchandising to discriminating San Franciscans. Although primarily devoted to women's fashions and cosmetics, I. Magnin also offers designer and high-quality merchandise for men and children.

MACY'S
Union Square / 397-3333

Whatever your whim — fancy chocolates, designer fashions or upscale cookery — you can find it at Macy's West, along with up-to-the-minute fashions for women and juniors. There are eight floors of fashion, jewelry, cosmetics and fragrances, accessories, home furnishings and housewares. Macy's East across the street has five floors of men's and children's clothing, and one of the largest electronics stores-within-a-store in the country.

NEIMAN MARCUS
Union Square / 362-3900

As a high-fashion specialty store, Neiman's carries well-known designer labels from around the world. The cosmetic and perfume department offers the finest skin care lines and fragrances available. The Rotunda Restaurant, under a spectacular stained glass dome, is a pleasant spot for lunch and afternoon tea.

NORDSTROM
San Francisco Shopping Centre / 243-8500
Stonestown Galleria / 753-1344

Occupying the top five floors of San Francisco Shopping Centre, Nordstrom places a special emphasis on fashion, including accessories and an incomparable selection of shoes. Styles for men, women and children range from contemporary classics and sportswear to the latest designer looks. Nordstrom's salespeople, noted for their friendliness and unparalleled service, will help with gift and wardrobe suggestions.
Open daily

SAKS FIFTH AVENUE
Union Square / 986-4300

San Francisco's Saks is a spacious, well-designed setting showcasing elegant and contemporary clothing and gifts for men, women and children. The circular floors and professional assistance make shopping here easy and enjoyable. From the Fifth Avenue Club Personal Shopping Service to Cafe SFA with its view of Union Square, this department store offers quality, service and the best of American and European fashion. Their spacious, comfortable salon pampers both men and women with a full array of beauty services.
Open daily

ACCESSORIES

BRAVA STRADA
3247 Sacramento St. at Presidio / 567-5757

Brava Strada displays its fine Italian, French and English accessories in an art gallery setting.

KATI KOOS
500 Sutter St. at Powell / 362-3437

At Kati Koos, customers can indulge themselves in specially selected pieces of wearable art and accessories. Sportswear and accessories by many local artists and designers are represented, as well as collections from around the country and the world. The styles combine fashion, fun and personal style with the friendly assistance of the owners. Shopping is a celebration at this whimsical gallery.
Closed Sunday

WALLIS
909 Sutter St. at Leavenworth / 775-9760

Small and quirky, Wallis specializes in unusual, affordable jewelry, plus hats, belts and small accessories.

JEWELRY

AMIR H. MOZAFFARIAN FINE JEWELRY
195 Post St. at Grant / 391-9995

Specializing in fine 18-karat and platinum jewelry, Amir H. Mozaffarian offers unique, customized pieces in contemporary and traditional designs. A fourth-generation jeweler, Amir H. Mozaffarian features the finest in jewelry, specializing in precious gems. The store also includes a collection of elegant Swiss watches by Piaget, Corum, Concord, and others. Personal service guaranteed. The store has been in business since 1883.
Closed Sunday

BAILEY BANKS & BIDDLE
Stonestown Galleria / 759-5310

Granat Bros. has joined Bailey Banks & Biddle in a venture offering the best in watches and diamonds. The store also features platinum, 14- and 18-karat gold jewelry and Lalique crystal.

ROLEX

Time's Golden Rulers:
Rolex Day-Date and Rolex Lady-Datejust

Twin classics of integrity and beauty, the Rolex Day-Date[R] and
Rolex Lady-Datejust[R] are superlative, self-winding chronometers,
each in 18kt. gold with matching President bracelet and pressure-
proof down to 330 feet with the renowned Oyster[R] case.

Only at your Official Rolex Jeweler.

sidney mobell
Designer and / Creator of Fine Jewelry

**ONE FINE STORE IN SAN FRANCISCO
LOBBY FAIRMONT HOTEL ATOP NOB HILL
950 MASON STREET (415)421-4747**

CERTIFIED ⅁⅁ GEMOLOGISTS • MEMBER AMERICAN GEM SOCIETY

BULGARI
Campton Place Hotel Kempinski
340 Stockton St., Suites 211 & 212 / 399-9141

This international jeweler from Italy is newly ensconsed in a warm and elegant shop on the second floor of the luxurious Campton Place Hotel. Bulgari is renowned for creating important as well as everyday jewelry, which combines colored precious and semi-precious stones with gold and alternative metals. The design, craftsmanship, detail and sheer beauty of each piece is without parallel. Enjoy personal and exclusive service as you choose from a distinctive collection of rings, bracelets, earrings, necklaces, brooches, pendants, cufflinks and men's and women's watches. Clients may also commission custom designs.
Closed Sunday

CARTIER, INC.
231 Post St. at Grant / 397-3180

Known worldwide for exquisite jewelry, Cartier is one of San Francisco's most admired shops. It is a fine setting for elegant jewelry, watches, silver, crystal and beautifully wrapped gifts.

GUMP'S
250 Post St. at Stockton / 982-1616

Internationally renowned for its unusual jewelry, Gump's has achieved its reputation by featuring one of the largest collections of freshwater pearls and fine jade jewelry in the United States. Gump's also carries beautiful pieces in colored stones such as lapis lazuli, tourmalines, aquamarines and coral.

MAXINE'S
3232 Sacramento St. at Presidio / 776-7160

If you appreciate the beauty and craftsmanship of artisans' jewelry, Maxine's is a gallery you shouldn't miss. Located in a renovated carriage room of an 1896 Victorian, the gallery itself is a jewel-toned setting in dark reds and greens. Dramatic interior lighting sets off the works of world-renowned artisans. Long-term exhibits have included the porcelain face pins of Roberta Hanson, the metals of Susan Silver Brown, beadwork by Lucia Antonelli and the fiber arts of Tina Johnson DePuy and Theodora Elston. You'll also discover new artists in limited monthly exhibits.
Closed Sunday

OPALS & GEMS OF AUSTRALIA
San Francisco Shopping Centre / 543-3160

Australia's only international jeweler carries one of the world's largest selections of gem quality opals.

PEARL OF ORIENT
900 North Point, Ghirardelli Square / 441-2288

Pearl of Orient imports its pearls directly from Japan and carries a complete line of pearl jewelry.

PROCTOR'S
141 Post St. at Grant / 395-9164

Proctor's offers the largest selection of Rolex watches in Northern California. A direct importer of both diamonds and pearls, Proctor's also has an exclusive collection of gold and gem jewelry.

SHAPUR
245 Post St. at Stockton / 392-1200

Every piece of jewelry at Shapur is unique and of the highest quality. Shapur also carries watches by Audemars Piguet, Blanc Pain, Breguet, Chopard, Gerald Genta, Girard Perregaux, Hublot, IWC, Jaeger le Coultre and Vacheron Constantin, among others.
Closed Sunday

SHREVE & CO.
200 Post St. at Grant / 421-2600

In business since 1852, Shreve & Co. is an architecturally unique store. Occupying one of the few buildings still standing after the 1906 earthquake, the prestigious jeweler is famous for its selection of the finest quality diamonds and colored stone jewelry, gold, pearls, giftware and name-brand watches (Rolex, Patek Philippe, Baume & Mercier, Cartier and Breitling). The store also carries an impressive collection of silver, crystal, stationery and giftware from around the world.
Closed Sunday

SIDNEY MOBELL
950 Mason St., Fairmont Hotel / 986-4747

Internationally renowned, Sidney Mobell has been seen on "The Tonight Show," "Lifestyles of the Rich and Famous," the CBS morning and evening news and ABC's "Good Morning America," and has been featured in magazines and newspapers around the world. He is also the creator of one-of-a-kind jewelry items such as the famous diamond Hourglass, diamond Mousetrap, Million Dollar Chess Set, Million Dollar Monopoly Set and Million Dollar Slot Machine. Sidney Mobell is an authorized agent for Rolex, Cartier, Patek Philippe, Audemars Piguet, Dupont, Mont Blanc and other fine names.
Closed Sunday

TIFFANY & CO.
352 Post St. at Powell / 781-7000

Tiffany & Co. lives up to its reputation for excellent quality in jewelry, watches, silver, china and crystal. From its extensive diamond and colored stone collections and internationally recognized designers — Elsa Peretti, Paloma Picasso and Jean Schlumberger — to its private stock china patterns, imported crystal and sterling silver flatware manufactured by its own craftsmen, Tiffany & Co. offers exclusive but diversified shopping.
Closed Sunday

COSTUME JEWELRY

IMPOSTORS
San Francisco Shopping Centre / 541-4922

You could even fool Liz and Zsa Zsa with these high-end copy jewels. Designs by Tiffany, Sidney Mobell and David Webb are meticulously recreated.

JEST JEWELS
2049 Union St. at Webster / 563-8839

A bright little store full of fun, inventive jewelry, Jest Jewels carries sterling silver as well as faux gems. The inventory is constantly changing, with the latest in earrings, pins, pendants, hats and watches from Europe and the United States.
Open daily

LA PARISIENNE
460 Post St. at Powell / 788-2255

When you enter this boutique, you are transported to the Paris of the 1890s — even the doors, counters and charming painted ceiling are original antiques. And what fun it is to feast your eyes on the unique costume jewelry owner Jola Anderson personally selects in Paris, including many one-of-a-kind pieces from designers not represented in any other American store. You will also find unusual gift items and a fabulous collection of antique posters and papers from "La Belle Epoque."
Closed Sunday

FURS

HERBERT'S FURS
180 Geary St. at Stockton / 397-9600

Herbert's has been a family concern since 1922. Frequent trips to Europe keep Herbert's abreast of fashion trends.

NEIMAN MARCUS FUR SALON
Union Square / 362-3900

In an intimate boutique atmosphere, customers are shown furs from around the world, most of which are created especially for this store.

REVILLON
Saks Fifth Ave., Union Square / 986-4300

The quality of a Revillon fur has been unparalleled for more than 250 years.

ROBERTS FURS
272 Post St. at Stockton / 362-6608

The elegant setting is the perfect atmosphere for presenting the finest mink, lynx, sable and fox.

SHOPPING

47

BALLY OF SWITZERLAND
238 Stockton St. at Maiden Lane / 398-7463

Fine quality leather and Italian workmanship blend beautifully in Bally's exclusive handbags, which coordinate with each season's shoe collection. The bags range from casual to very dressy, with a special line for men that includes an alligator clutch, shoulder bag and attache case. Small carry-on bags and briefcases of the softest leather comprise the luggage line.
Open daily

BOTTEGA VENETA
108 Geary St. at Grant / 981-1700

This fabled leather goods house from Italy is the place to go for the ultimate in self-indulgence. Every season's collection features a different theme. The quality and excellence which go into the handcrafting of every Bottega Veneta product are reflected in the glorious colors and materials. The warmth of the store highlights the handbags, as well as Bottega Veneta's beautiful luggage, briefcases, small leather goods and other accessories.
Closed Sunday

BREE
San Francisco Shopping Centre / 957-0998

Internationally respected German designer Wolf Peter Bree is well known for his natural cowhide bags. Bree's collection features dyed leather as well.

THE COACH STORE
190 Post St. at Grant / 392-1772

Coach's luxe handbags, made from smooth, full-grain leather in rich colors with solid brass detailing, are renowned for their clean, classic styling and quality workmanship.

EL PORTAL
San Francisco Shopping Centre / 896-5637

Established in 1936, El Portal, the "First Family of Fine Leathergoods," has brought a large collection from the world's leading manufacturers in luggage, handbags, business cases and unique gifts to San Francisco.

THE GUCCI SHOP
One Union Square
200 Stockton St. at Geary / 392-2808

Gucci, one of the most prestigious names in international fashion, carries an elegant selection of men's and women's apparel, leather goods and accessories. Both the fashions and leather goods share a legacy of quality and style.
Open daily

HERMES
One Union Square
212 Stockton St. at Geary / 391-7200

In 1837 Thierry Hermes opened his first leather goods shop in Paris and began a tradition of excellence and craftsmanship that has made Hermes world-famous. Today, the Hermes line includes silk ties and scarves, sportswear for men and women, fragrance, jewelry, home furnishings and, of course, exquisite leather items.
Open daily

LOUIS VUITTON
230 Post St. at Grant / 391-6200
I. Magnin, Union Square / 788-4856

Louis Vuitton's timeless styling of luggage and travel accessories is matched only by its dedication to unparalleled craftsmanship. Since 1854, Louis Vuitton luggage, made for enduring elegance, has been the traveling companion of celebrities, government figures and royalty. The company will manufacture trunks and selected items to order.
Open daily

MALM LUGGAGE
222 Grant Ave. at Sutter / 392-0417

Established in 1860, Malm Luggage consistently offers exquisite luggage and leather goods. Designer lines include Tumi, Boyt, Hartmann, Ghurka, Gold Pfeil, Holland Sport and French of California to mention a few. The luggage is made from full-grain leather and is also available in exotic leathers and nylons. The store carries business cases, travel accessories and such luxury items as Mont Blanc pens. Malm Luggage offers full repair service, free monogramming and free giftwrapping.
Open daily

MARK CROSS
170 Post St. at Grant / 391-7770

Few companies can lay claim to a heritage that crosses international boundaries with more than 140 years of success. The leather goods are all hand-cut and hand-constructed of calfskin, pigskin, lizard and ostrich.
Closed Sunday

MCM
343 Powell St. at Post / 989-0626

Designer Michael Cromer of Munich introduced his exclusive line of hand-crafted bags and luggage to San Francisco in 1987. Available only at I. Magnin and at MCM boutiques, the trademark designs with the MCM logo are well known in Europe and come in a basic sporty brown, a summer-season white and a subtle black suitable for evening use.
Open daily

OPTICAL

CITY OPTIX
2154 Chestnut St. at Steiner / 921-1188

San Francisco's most exciting eyewear can be found in this plush, modern store where an in-house optometrist and outstanding service make selecting glasses pure fun.

EYES IN DISGUISE
2189 Union St. at Fillmore / 474-5321

For creative, exciting eyewear, Eyes in Disguise is the place to go. You'll find an extensive collection of frames and sunglasses from Europe, personally selected by the owners every year to reflect the latest trends in eyewear fashion. Cosmetic opticians help you create a perfect balance between your best features and distinctive frames. Skilled technicians then conduct a series of precise inspections of your glasses to guarantee unsurpassed quality and comfort.
Open daily

INVISION
1907 Fillmore St. at Pine / 563-9003

Trained opticians provide the most careful service at Invision, and will complete most prescriptions while you wait. Eyewear ranges from classic to provocative.

MIR OPTICS
628 California St. at Kearny / 433-9338

One of the most beautiful optical stores in San Francisco, Mir Optics has a soothing, elegant ambiance created by cherrywood and a minimalist decor. Alex Arrais, a licensed dispensing optician, has introduced a different concept in purchasing eyewear. Instead of offering a few styles from a hodge-podge of manufacturers, he dedicates distinct display areas to the entire collection of top eyewear designers. You'll find more than 200 frames from Oliver Peoples, the full range of designs from Issey Miyake, Bada and Armani, and a large variety of Persol sunglasses. The service is as personal and distinctive as the store itself.
Open daily

THE OCULARIUM
2035 Union St. at Webster / 929-9400
2336 Chestnut St. at Divisadero / 563-2475

For a contemporary look, the Ocularium is just what you would hope to find. Here, you'll see the difference between glasses and fine designer eyewear.

RIMS & GOGGLES
445 Sutter St. at Powell / 397-6511

Eighteen years in competitive San Francisco attest to the

SHOPPING

success of Rims & Goggles. Exclusive to the shop is a fine selection of designer frames from Europe.

SPECTACLES OF UNION SQUARE
177 Maiden Lane at Stockton / 781-8556

All name labels are stocked, and contact lenses are available for immediate delivery. A full-time staff technician is on hand and there is one-hour service for emergencies.

SUN SHADE
900 North Point, Ghirardelli Square / 673-1224
San Francisco Shopping Centre / 543-7967
188 O'Farrell St. near Macy's / 291-9890
Embarcadero Center Four / 788-2279

No one walks out of Sun Shade without a new pair of sunglasses, no matter what their budget. From inexpensive copies to the real thing by Giorgio Armani, Laura Biagiotti, Porsche Design, Persol and Oakley, Sun Shade has a 1,200-frame selection at great prices.
Open daily

HATS

COUP DE CHAPEAU
1906 Fillmore St. at Bush / 931-7793

Coup de Chapeau carries custom headgear for all occasions, whether you seek attention or the anonymity of Garbo. Jenifer Mathieu designs tempting felt, straw and flowered hats in haute-couture, fantasy and classic styles for both men and women.
Closed Sunday & Monday

HATS ON POST
210 Post St. at Grant, 2nd floor / 392-3737

For that "So Very San Francisco" look in reasonably priced, contemporary headwear, stop by Hats on Post. Choose from a wide selection of felt, straw, fur, bridal and cocktail hats by well-known designers, or have owner Sheryl Krajewski create a hat just for you. She also custom designs bridal hats and veils.
Closed Sunday

READY-TO-WEAR FOR MEN & WOMEN

BANANA REPUBLIC
256 Grant Ave. at Sutter / 788-3087

Banana Republic is well known for its classic, comfortable, natural-fiber clothing for travel.

BEBE
1954 Union St. at Buchanan / 563-BEBE

Bebe offers redefined classic styles at exceptional prices. The stores feature blazers, vests, skirts, trousers, and private-label separates and accessories.

CIGNAL
San Francisco Shopping Centre / 979-0209
Stonestown Galleria / 566-3562

Some of the freshest names in modern clothing for men and women — Casual Equip, Maxwear, Girbaud, DeNimes, MDG, Marabou, Max Studio and Nina K — can be found at Cignal.

CLUB MONACO
San Francisco Shopping Centre / 243-9707

Exciting and innovative, Club Monaco's flagship store is a one-stop source for a wide range of timeless, popularly priced casual apparel and accessories.

DEAN'S
2238 Fillmore St. at Clay / 928-4288

This select boutique features better fashions for women, including cocktail wear, leather outfits, career dress and sportswear. Mr. Jax, Bill Blass, Stizzoli and Sue Wong are some of the collections offered. A full line of accessories is also available.
Open daily

GO SILK
424 Sutter St. at Powell / 391-2474

If you like silk but don't like to take care of it, you'll love the washable silk classics sold here. The luxurious sportswear features timeless shapes and streamlined silhouettes in a range of silk blends. Go Silk is an international fashion label, and this store is the first in the country to feature its collection exclusively. It's the perfect place for those who want a designer look in easy-care fabrics — there's even washable linen!
Open daily

J. CREW
San Francisco Shopping Centre / 546-6262

In the spirit of their renowned catalog, J. Crew's signature color, comfort and style are also captured in their San Francisco retail store.

JOAN VASS
359 Sutter St. at Stockton / 433-7913

Joan Vass clothing is so comfortable, durable and timeless that it inspires lifelong devotion. No one throws out an old Joan Vass outfit — it would be sacrilege. Instead, fans replenish their collection of cotton cashmere knit separates and mix and match them in new combinations that always look fresh and fashionable. This New York designer, famous for her unconfining waistbands and subtle colors, also offers a smaller collection for men. The colors change seasonally, giving women *or* men who haven't yet been seduced by the Joan Vass style of comfort many chances to become devotees.
Closed Sunday

MAC
812 Post St. at Leavenworth / 775-2515

MAC showcases upcoming designers, both American and international, including Hank Ford and Todd Oldham. Sportswear, evening clothes and at-home wear are a main feature.

NICOLE MILLER
50 Post St., Crocker Galleria / 398-3111

You'll find the complete Nicole Miller Limited Edition Collection of whimsical silk ties, scarves, vests, shirts, shoes, handbags and her "ultimate" little black dresses.

OPERETTA
900 North Point, Ghirardelli Square / 928-4676

Casual wear does not begin to describe the one-of-a-kind Italian designs Anne-Marie Gatti buys from artisans in Northern Italy. All are of such high quality that you'll blink when you see the price tags.

OVERLAND SHEEPSKIN CO.
21 Grant Ave. at O'Farrell / 296-9180

The Overland Sheepskin Co. presents traditional designs in a captivating setting of tan adobe walls, pressed tin ceiling and rustic plank floors. Anything that can be made of sheepskin or fleece is available here, from elegant mouton coats and curly lamb vests to sturdy jackets, slippers, rugs, car seat covers — even baby blankets. Leather jackets, sportswear and Australian oilskin raincoats round out the well-priced selection. Another branch can be found in Yountville in the Napa Valley.
Open daily

SPICE BY LEXIES
3505 California St. at Locust / 931-1899

Lexies features contemporary women's fashions by Joan Vass and Bettina Ridel. Fashions by these designers, as well as Luna — the store's private label — and shoes are available here.
Open daily

UKO
2070 Union St. at Webster / 563-0330

Those who appreciate the originality and quality of contemporary Japanese clothing should take a look at UKO. The store carries several established designers from Japan, with an emphasis on versatile, unique and well-priced clothing for both men and women.
Open daily

LEATHER FASHIONS

BALLY OF SWITZERLAND
238 Stockton St. at Maiden Lane / 398-7463

Known for its shoes and handbags, Bally has an equally impressive line of lightweight leather clothing for men

SHOPPING

and women. You'll find sweaters with suede or leather trim, and leather and suede jackets, all made in Italy in classic colors and styles.
Open daily

DUDLEY PERKINS COMPANY
66 Page St. at Market / 703-9477

The world's oldest Harley-Davidson Dealership is also the purveyor of some of the most popular leather fashions available. Designed for riders but just as coveted for their fashion appeal, the jackets, vests, pants and boots are practical, rugged and superbly crafted of top-grade leather. That's not all you'll find in this fabulous store. Shirts in every style, denim and cotton jackets, pants, socks, hats, accessories, gift items of all kinds, even boxer shorts and children's clothing, all bear the trademark Harley-Davidson wings or logo. Dudley Perkins is a shopping haven for the motorcycle buff and anyone else who appreciates long-wearing quality and design.
Closed Sunday

NORTH BEACH LEATHER
1365 Columbus Ave. at Beach / 441-3208
190 Geary St. at Stockton / 362-8300

The in-house designs of Michael Hoban are internationally recognized. With close connections to New York and Europe, the classic, clean-cut modern lines of their apparel reflect an eye to fashion direction. Their luxurious lambskin jackets, pants and dresses are thin, lightweight and durable.
Open daily

TANNERY WEST
San Francisco Shopping Centre / 227-0140

"Leather in style" is the motto here. Tannery West offers a private line of elegant styles made of European leathers vat-dyed in rich, warm hues.

SWEATERS

DREAMWEAVER
171 Maiden Lane / 981-2040
Pier 39 / 433-3571

After 12 years in business, Dreamweaver has gained a reputation as *the* source in the Bay Area for beautiful and unique handknit sweaters. You'll find a huge selection in wool, cotton, angora, mohair, alpaca and silk. Featured are the famous Berek line of handknits, Coogi of Australia, Christine Foley and Southwool.
Closed Sunday on Maiden Lane; Pier 39 open daily

I.B. DIFFUSION
San Francisco Shopping Centre / 543-7713

Those who know I.B. Diffusion as pioneers in embellished sweaters will be pleased by the full collection assembled in its San Francisco store.

THE KILKENNY SHOP
900 North Point, Ghirardelli Square / 771-8984

Everything here is imported from Ireland and is either handknit or handwoven.

SCOTCH HOUSE
187 Post St. at Grant / 391-1264

Scotch House's exclusive clothing includes a fine selection of pure Scottish cashmeres, lambswool and merino sweaters from the United States and Irish handknits.

THREE BAGS FULL
2181 Union St. at Fillmore / 567-5753
500 Sutter St. at Powell / 398-SWTR

Three Bags Full shouldn't be missed if you have a passion for sweaters. Handmade in luscious fibers and colors, these original sweaters for men, women and children line the walls all the way up to a skylit balcony where socks and leather accessories are also featured.
Open daily; Sutter St. store closed Sunday

TSE CASHMERE
171 Post St. at Grant / 391-1112

Plush cashmere sportswear collections designed for men, women and children make comfortable day-to-evening dressing easy.

OUTDOOR OUTFITTERS

BOGNER
400 Sutter St. at Stockton / 434-3888

Bogner, a European fashion label, has been in the forefront of the sportswear and skiwear market for 57 years.

CANTERBURY OF NEW ZEALAND
89 Maiden Lane at Grant / 781-3311

Canterbury's rugged rugby and yachting-inspired clothing has become the preferred gear of sportsmen (and women) around the world.

DON SHERWOOD'S GOLF & TENNIS WORLD
320 Grant Ave. at Sutter / 989-5000

At Don Sherwood's, you'll find three gigantic floors filled with the finest sports equipment, including the largest selection of golf and tennis equipment on the West Coast.

EDDIE BAUER
220 Post St. at Grant / 986-7600
Stonestown Galleria / 664-9262
Village of Corte Madera / 927-1813

Comfortable shoes, clothing and protection from the elements are all here. Eddie Bauer has been outfitting people for more than 60 years.

Ghirardelli Square

Sutter at Market

THE SHARPER IMAGE® STORES

Your source for unique gifts.

Corte Madera
The Village
(415) 924-7749

Santa Clara
Valley Fair Mall
(408) 241-9290

San Francisco
Davis at Broadway
(415) 445-6100

Sutter at Market
(415) 398-6472

Ghirardelli Square
(415) 776-1443

Carmel
Ocean Avenue
between Mission
and Junipero
(408) 626-0393

FTC SKI AND SPORTS
1586 Bush St. at Franklin / 673-8363

FTC offers a complete line of equipment and apparel for skiing, tennis, rollerskating, snowboarding and skateboarding. For the skier, they feature K2, Rossignol, Volkl, Spyder, Salomon, Dynamic and RD. For those whose interests take them to the courts, FTC offers Prince, Wilson and Head.
Open daily

ORVIS
300 Grant Ave. at Sutter / 392-1600

Men and women who demand classic good looks in sportswear have been coming to Orvis since 1856. The clothes are tailored to move easily and wear well.

TIMBERLAND AT RIA'S
900 North Point, Ghirardelli Square / 771-4393
437 Sutter St., Grand Hyatt on Union Square / 398-0895

Timberland's ready-to-wear collection is showcased at Ria's. The best materials, including waterproof washable leather, cotton, wool and nylon, are used in the collection, which can take you from Mount Everest to Wall Street. Classically styled handknit sweaters, pants, shirts, jackets and even socks are made to withstand the elements and look great for years to come. Leather caps, handbags and accessories are also available. And, of course, the complete shoe and boot line for men and women is available here, as well as the famous Alden shoes, made in New England.
Open daily

CLASSIC WEAR FOR WOMEN

BROOKS BROTHERS FOR WOMEN
201 Post St. at Grant / 397-4500

Whatever kind of busy schedule you may have, you will always find a well-tailored suit, coat or dress, the classic skirt or slacks, or a choice of colorful shirts, sweaters and accessories at Brooks Brothers.

BURBERRYS OF LONDON
225 Post St. at Grant / 392-2200

Burberrys' classic look has enthusiasts worldwide. The famous Burberrys trenchcoat is joined by coordinated accessories such as scarves, handbags and luggage, and suits and sweaters for the working woman. Expert alterations and fittings are guaranteed by tailors on staff.
Open daily

CELINE
155 Post St. at Grant / 397-1140

Madame Celine entered the fashion world in 1947 with a line of shoes that launched her company into immediate success. Accessories such as bags, travel goods, scarves and jewelry were followed by classic fashion

designs of ready-to-wear sportswear and evening clothes.
Open daily

LAURA ASHLEY
253 Post St. at Grant / 788-0190
1827 Union St. at Octavia / 922-7200

Laura Ashley, recognized worldwide for her romantic fashions and country-inspired home furnishings, is firmly established with more than 130 shops in the United States alone. A wide choice of printed fabrics, wall coverings, women's and children's dresses and skirts round out the Laura Ashley look.
Open daily

MADRIGAL
590 Sutter St. at Mason / 989-3478

Madrigal offers the finest quality clothing for women who like a tailored look.

PORTS INTERNATIONAL
San Francisco Shopping Centre / 896-0408

Classics with fashion flair are the cachet of this top quality Canadian label.

SAN FRANCISCO PENDLETON
464 Sutter St. at Powell / 788-6383

Pendleton's separates and sportswear all share the classic lines and quality production this venerable Oregon company is known for.

DESIGNER WEAR FOR WOMEN

ADRIENNE VITTADINI
San Francisco Shopping Centre / 777-3440

Adrienne Vittadini's three lines — Collection, Sport and Dresses — are displayed in a sleek Italian-style boutique.

AVANT PREMIERE
1942 Fillmore St. at Pine / 673-8875

"The little Paris in the heart of San Francisco," Avant Premiere has a collection you won't find anywhere else. The owner travels all over the world to select styles from classic to high fashion. Attention is paid to fabrics, such as cashmere, tweed, wool, viscose and silk, that are right for the office, and prices that are manageable on a salary. Personal service is another specialty.
Open daily

CHANEL BOUTIQUE
155 Maiden Lane at Stockton / 981-1550

Take one step into this elegant boutique and you'll know why the name Chanel epitomizes style and elegance. The interior is beige and black — Coco Chanel's signature combination — and three floors, linked by a curving, mirrored staircase, showcase Chanel's entire ready-to-wear collection, from evening gowns and outerwear to bathing suits and the famous belts and bags. Customers are pampered by San Francisco's finest salespeople, who will serve refreshments, coordinate and accessorize your wardrobe, then put you in the hands of the resident makeup artist. *Open daily*

DIAGONALE
352 Sutter St. at Grant / 397-3633

With an interior designed by one of Italy's foremost architects, and a staff chosen for its talent and experience, Diagonale is a boutique dedicated to bringing the best men's and women's European designer fashions to San Francisco. The collections carried reflect this ideal: Claude Montana, Thierry Mugler, Istante, Moschino, Iceberg and Jean Paul Gaultier, to name a few. Diagonale is located one block from Union Square.
Closed Sunday

DIANA SLAVIN WOMENSWEAR
3 Claude Lane near Sutter / 677-9939

Look no further for fabulous separates — pants, skirts, blouses and jackets — that are superbly tailored and cut to fit a woman's body and lifestyle.

EMPORIO ARMANI
One Grant Ave. at O'Farrell / 677-9400

Emporio Armani carries Giorgio Armani's state-of-the-art clothing, shoes and accessories. You'll find everything from elegant dresses to jeans, including a dizzying choice of Armani jackets.

ESCADA
259 Post St. btwn. Stockton & Grant / 391-3500

The beautiful, three-level boutique with dramatic circular staircase carries German-based Escada, Laurel and Crisca labels, along with Escada leather goods and Beaute fragrances.

GEORGIOU
1725 Union St. at Gough / 776-8144
2800 Leavenworth St., The Anchorage / 441-3301

Georgiou addresses every woman's need for a versatile wardrobe that never goes out of style.

GIANNI VERSACE FOR WOMEN
70 Post St., Crocker Galleria / 956-7977

Gianni Versace's complete collection for women is available here. One of the most respected and innovative designers, Versace has an international following, including many famous performers. He now has a network of more than 100 boutiques worldwide. Each season, Versace does extensive research that leads to the introduction of unique and beautiful fabrics. This original approach to fabric, combined with Versace's innate sense of proportion and a certain flamboyance, results in designs that are both new and classic.
Closed Sunday

SHOPPING

Mondiella

393 Sutter Street

San Francisco, CA 94108
Tel: (415) 788-7918
Fax: (415) 788-6608

THE GROCERY STORE
1372 Burlingame Ave., Burlingame / 348-1372

A woman who prizes designer wear won't mind driving to Burlingame for these fashions. Newly opened, The Grocery Store showcases specialty clothing, shoes and accessories, with a special highlighted every week. The boutique features high-fashion clothing, as well as not-so-serious items, all selected by the owners of Susan. With stores in San Francisco and Burlingame, they choose designs for the woman who wants just the right look yet appreciates fashion with a sense of fun. *Closed Sunday*

HERMES
One Union Square
212 Stockton St. at Geary / 391-7200

In 1837 Thierry Hermes opened his first leather goods shop in Paris and began a long tradition of acclaim. The French firm is now among the world's finest luxury goods houses, creating exquisite silk scarves, leather items, clothing, fragrances and home furnishings. *Open daily*

JASMINE CURTIS
402 Sutter St. at Stockton / 956-8080

Whether you choose a black, gold or white creation, every garment is made from hand-beaded, imported silk and each design is guaranteed not to fade from memory.

JEANNE-MARC
262 Sutter St. at Grant / 362-1121

San Francisco designers Jeanne Allen and Marc Grant produce a trademark line characterized by a striking mix of colors and patterns.

JESSICA MCCLINTOCK
353 Sutter St. at Grant / 397-0987

Jessica McClintock's designs in lace, satin and silk are pretty and feminine. Her trademark touches prevail, with softly sculpted fabrics and graceful flourishes.

JIM-ELLE
2237 Fillmore St. at Sacramento / 567-9500

Women's designer wear for the casual lifestyle fills this spacious, bright boutique. The best from the collections of Matsuda, Go Silk and Harriet Selwyn, among others, is put together in creative, individual combinations by a most professional staff. *Open daily*

JOLIN
Embarcadero Three, lobby level / 982-5622

Jolin is a European odyssey into the world of high fashion. Designed for successful women who desire avant-garde fashions, the luscious Italian silk dresses, hand-knitted and beaded sweaters, soft Parisian leathers

and suedes, summer linens and stunning accessories
will take you from boardroom to opening night in style.
Closed Sunday

JUSTINE
3600 Sacramento St. at Locust / 921-8548

Justine purchases her collection in Paris and sells it
directly to her customers in a shop with genuine French
ambiance. Well-known designer lines include Georges
Rech and Synonyme, as well as knitwear by Dorothee Bis
and Fabrice Karel. These collections are complemented
by accessories from Georges Rech and Catherine Prevost.
Justine also carries a fine line of handbags.
Closed Sunday & Monday

LAISE ADZER
360 Sutter St. at Stockton / 981-3505

Laise Adzer, a tradition in ethnic dressing since 1979,
embodies a collection of original styles and accessories
adapted from all over the globe. This dressing
approach transcends the world of ready-to-wear and
features such distinctive fabrics as silk, ikat, African
kinte cloth and various handwoven Middle Eastern
rayons. Laise Adzer's home furnishings complement
its ambiance of cultural chic.
Closed Sunday

MARIMEKKO
50 Post St., Crocker Galleria / 392-1742

From Finland come Marimekko's universally appealing
women's fashions and textile designs. The boutique carries a seasonal collection of the finest cotton and wool
apparel, as well as silk-screened cotton fabrics.
Marimekko also offers much more — distinctive handwoven cotton jackets by Annikki Karvinen, fine sterling
silver jewelry by Lapponia, refined leather shoulder bags
and versatile cotton totes, pillows for the home and a
generous selection of Finnish art glass and handicrafts.
Closed Sunday

MAXMARA
175 Post St. at Grant / 981-0900

Famous in Italy, the MaxMara line is known for fabric
quality and elegant detail. As the first retail boutique in
the United States, MaxMara carries subsidiary lines as
well: evening wear by Pianoforte; updated classics by
Penny Black; innovative, fun styles by Sportmax; and
casual classics by Weekend.
Closed Sunday

MONDI
San Francisco Shopping Centre / 546-9525
50 Post St., Crocker Galleria / 781-4604

Known for the simple elegance of its styling and the luxurious quality of its fabrics, Germany's Mondi evolves
new themes for every collection, coordinating each

JOLIN
FINE WOMEN'S APPAREL

THREE EMBARCADERO CENTER

LOBBY LEVEL

415-982-5622

detail for a mix-and-match wardrobe as individual as its wearer. You'll find classic shades as well as subdued colors, neutral hues and tone-on-tone effects, and fabrics ranging from Mondi's famous knits to feathery light silks. Mondi's head-to-toe accessories include shoes, bags, scarves and even color-coordinated belts.
Open daily at San Francisco Shopping Centre; closed Sunday at Crocker Galleria

MONDIELLA
393 Sutter St. at Stockton / 788-7918

Mondiella gears its designer wear to successful women who desire avant-garde fashion. You'll find the best from the collections of Gianfranco Ferre, Moschino, Genny, Teadora Teadora, KL by Karl Lagerfeld, Giorgio Armani and Versace. Mondiella also carries a collection of accessories from Italy and Paris. Current fashions are put together in creative individual combinations by a professional staff, making shopping here effortless and time-saving.
Open daily

OBIKO
794 Sutter St. at Jones / 775-2882

Sandra Sakata works with Bay Area artists, designers and craftsmen who create handwoven, hand-knitted and handpainted individual designs with a feminine flavor. Most pieces are unconstructed, designed to project the wearer's style, mood and personality. One-of-a-kind accessories are equally sensational.
Closed Sunday

PELUCHE
3366 Sacramento St. at Walnut / 346-6361

With a unique approach to customer relations that includes a comfortable sitting area, complimentary white wine or mineral water, and a consulting service, Peluche is a small boutique packed with exclusive European fashions in silk, linen, jersey, knit and other fine fabrics. Peluche provides a consistent image of understated elegance for day and evening wear.
Closed Sunday

POLO/RALPH LAUREN
90 Post St., Crocker Galleria / 567-POLO

A one-stop location in San Francisco for the entire family collection of famed American designer Ralph Lauren, this store's elegant, multilevel interior features womenswear, including activewear, sportcoats, accessories, footwear and suits. Personalized service is a key asset of this must-see store, with a home furnishings department in the same location.
Closed Sunday

SUSAN
3685 Sacramento St. at Spruce / 922-3685
1403 Burlingame Ave., Burlingame / 347-0452

If you want sophisticated contemporary classics, tailored with a sense of fun and individualism, you will find them at the Susan stores. Combining the best in European and Japanese fashions, the selection of designers includes Jean Paul Gaultier, Barbara Bui, Helmut Lang, Comme des Garcons, Yohji Yamamoto, Ozbek, Moschino and Versace. Susan's expert staff helps accessorize the outfits, from shoes by Robert Clergerie and Stephane Kelian to jewelry by Steve Vaubel and handbags and belts by such designers as Christian Lacroix and Moschino.
Closed Sunday

VERSUS GIANNI VERSACE
50 Post St., Crocker Galleria / 616-0600

Renowned Italian designer Gianni Versace's long-awaited second line for women and men can be found in the new Versus boutique. It's a young, sexy collection, with Versace's trademark quality, fabric and workmanship but prices far below his couture collection. You'll find sportswear, leather, evening wear and an extensive line of accessories, from belts and bags to shoes and fragrance.
Closed Sunday

WILKES BASHFORD
375 Sutter St. at Stockton / 986-4380

Wilkes Bashford has five fabulous floors to browse, with women's and men's clothes alternating from area to area. Designers include Karl Lagerfeld, Jean-Louis Scherrer, Chloe, Thierry Mugler, Issey Miyake, Jean Muir and Richard Tyler.

LINGERIE

ARICIE
50 Post St., Crocker Galleria / 989-0261

In a setting at once intimate and elegant, Aricie offers the finest in lingerie. Fabrics featured are exquisite silks for luxury, cool cottons for comfort and the latest easy-care "microfibers" for convenience. Aricie's friendly, knowledgeable staff will help you select from the range of sexy garments, from slithery Harlow-like gowns and tailored Hepburn-type silk pajamas to exotic bustiers and teddy-thongs a la Madonna. Most bras and garter belts are imports from Italy and France and include such names as La Perla, Chantal Thomass, Aubade and Rien (French for "nothing"!). An extensive line of hosiery, including hard-to-find silk stockings, complements the beautiful lingerie.
Closed Sunday

TOUJOURS
2484 Sacramento St. at Fillmore / 346-3988

This small, pale peach-and-aqua shop showcases individual designers of intimate apparel. Featured are bras by La Perla, Chantal Thomass, Lejaby and Lou, silk chiffon by Frances Smiley and linen by such designers as Erica

SHOPPING

Tanov. Cottons are big at Toujours, and the best European and domestic lines, including Hanro, Ripcosa and Calida, are represented, as is Michelle Nicole Wesley, who designs in cotton exclusively. Toujours also carries basics from slips and stockings to garter belts and is expanding to include accessories such as hats, one-of-a-kind slippers and an outstanding collection of designer and antique jewelry.
Open daily

VICTORIA'S SECRET
395 Sutter St. at Stockton / 397-0521

Victoria's Secret is a romantic boutique that captures the ambiance of a Victorian boudoir. Other locations are in Stonestown Galleria and San Francisco Shopping Centre.

MATERNITY

JAPANESE WEEKEND (JWO)
864 Post St. at Hyde / 775-1529

Designers of the famous Obi Kutsurogi maternity waistband ("OK" for short), JWO has skirts, pants, tops and dresses that can take you through nine months in the utmost comfort and style.

MOTHERHOOD MATERNITY BOUTIQUE
San Francisco Shopping Centre / 227-0825

With more than 25 years in business and 350 locations nationwide, Motherhood offers maternity fashion in active wear to evening wear. Maternity fashions at Motherhood are from the finest fabrics and include clothing for career women, tops, skirts, dresses and maternity lingerie — everything to help women look and feel their best during pregnancy.
Open daily

MOTHERS WORK MATERNITY
125 Geary St. at Stockton / 397-3900

Mothers Work leads the way in comfortable clothing for the professional mother-to-be.

PAGE BOY MATERNITY
372 Sutter St. at Stockton / 986-5334

Together with suits and dresses for career women, Page Boy carries sportswear, lingerie and evening wear.

WOMEN'S SHOES

ARTHUR BEREN SHOES
222 Stockton St. at Maiden Lane / 397-8900

With more than 40 years' experience, Arthur Beren Shoes selects only the finest footwear and accessories from designers and manufacturers from around the world. In the San Francisco spirit, the selection emphasizes superbly comfortable walking shoes and quietly elegant footwear for dress or business. Their spacious, two-level store offers a wide range of

sizes, styles and colors for both men and women. Shoes by Arche, Mephisto, Cole-Haan, Joan and David, Amalfi, Stuart Weitzman, Bruno Magli, Yves St. Laurent and many other designers are featured. The store has the largest collection of Salvatore Ferragamo offered anywhere in the United States. It also carries matching handbags by Ferragamo, as well as elegant bags by DeVecci, Rodo and Pierotucci.
Open daily

BALLY OF SWITZERLAND
238 Stockton St. at Maiden Lane / 398-7463

A favorite of European women for more than two decades, Bally is synonymous with the best in shoes. You won't find these supple, elegant creations anywhere else in San Francisco. From classic loafers to dressy heels, the Bally of Switzerland shoe collection offers style and comfort that last and last.
Open daily

BRUNO MAGLI
285 Geary St. at Powell / 421-0356

Completely done in blond wood and marble imported from Italy, Bruno Magli shows Magli's Salon collection, which has a much more European look than Bruno Magli styles available elsewhere. Shoes range from sporty to dressy in sizes 4 to 11, all widths. Also available are leather accessories for men and women and leather skirts and jackets for women.
Open daily

FRANK MORE
105 Grant Ave. at Geary / 421-0356

Frank More specializes in very fine quality men's and women's shoes and boots. Some shoes are designed exclusively for the store, others are from an excellent selection imported from Italy, with matching belts and bags.
Open daily

GIMME SHOES
868 Post St. at Hyde / 928-6677

Although somewhat off the shopper's beaten path, Gimme Shoes has been discovered by those searching for innovative European styling for men and women.

JOAN & DAVID
172 Geary St. at Stockton / 397-1958

One of the first Joan & David boutiques in the country, the shoe salon on Union Square carries all your favorite styles. The designs are ultrafashionable and classy, with loafers, sandals and dressier styles meant for year-round wear.
Open daily

KENNETH COLE
2078 Union St. at Webster / 346-2161
San Francisco Shopping Centre / 227-4536

The very modern and spacious interiors showcase a full line of men's and women's Italian crafted shoes, leather handbags and accessories.

MARAOLO
404 Sutter St. at Stockton / 781-0895

Maraolo has made quality shoes for designers such as Armani in the Maraolo family factory. The San Francisco store also has handbags, belts and attaches.

SHAW FASHION SHOES
2001 Union St. at Buchanan / 922-5676

At Shaw, you can find designer shoes for a professional image at the office, casual shoes for the weekend and nightlife shoe fashions for formal affairs.

TIMBERLAND AT RIA'S
900 North Point, Ghirardelli Square / 771-4393
437 Sutter St., Grand Hyatt on Union Square / 398-0895

Ria's carries the whole line of outdoor Timberland shoes, apparel and accessories, including handbags and luggage, for men and women. The handsewn, waterproof shoes are designed with both function and good looks in mind. Timberland also designs sophisticated flats suitable for play and office wear. Ria's also has a wide selection of colorful Sebago Docksiders, loafers, western boots, Indian mocassins and those wonderfully comfortable latex-sealed Arche shoes and Mephistos from France, as well as many other famous brands, including Alden shoes made in New England, which make shopping at Ria's unique.
Open daily

22 STEPS
280 Sutter St. at Grant / 398-7797

Shoe designers for women include Robert Clergerie, Phillipe Model, Make-Up, Sybilla, Rene Caty and Luc Berjen. Along with shoes come unusual accessories.

CLASSIC WEAR FOR MEN

ALFRED DUNHILL OF LONDON
290 Post St. at Stockton / 781-3368

In 1907, Alfred Dunhill began as a tobacconist, specializing in hand-rolled cigars and custom-blended pipe tobacco. Today, the quality of the tobacco and accessories remains the best. Dunhill has added a splendid line of classic men's clothing that includes sportswear, sports coats, ties, shirts, sweaters and luggage.
Open daily

VERSUS

Gianni Versace

AQUASCUTUM
340 Post St. at Stockton
Bullock & Jones, 3rd floor / 392-5633

The London-based shop provided Humphrey Bogart with his Casablanca trenchcoat. In addition to the "Bogart" and other fine outerwear, Aquascutum offers classic clothing and accessories for men and women.

BROOKS BROTHERS FOR MEN
201 Post St. at Grant / 397-4500

Henry Brooks introduced the button-down collar in the early 1900s and produced a full range of traditional clothing made from material noted for quality, appearance and long wear.
Open daily

BULLOCK & JONES
340 Post St. on Union Square / 392-4243

Since 1853, Bullock & Jones has offered classic clothing, shoes and luggage and well-known brands such as Oxxford, Zegna, Hickey-Freeman, Chester Barrie, Aquascutum of London and Bally of Switzerland.

CABLE CAR CLOTHIERS
246 Sutter St. at Grant / 397-4740

Cable Car Clothiers is a solidly traditional men's store, in San Francisco since 1939, featuring British goods and accessories made from the finest natural fibers.

HASTINGS
101 Post St. at Kearny / 393-8900
331 Powell St., Westin St. Francis Hotel / 393-8910

In business since 1854, Hastings carries designer labels including Hart Schaffner & Marx, Hickey-Freeman, Austin-Reed and Canali for men, and Barrie Pace and Ellen Tracy for women.

THE HOUND
111 Sutter St. at Montgomery / 989-0429
275 Battery St. at Sacramento / 982-1578

Located next to the Crocker Galleria, this comfortable shop features quality clothing ranging from formalwear to sportswear, including such names as Norman Hilton, Robert Talbott, Gitman Bros., Ike Behar, Kenneth Gordon, Samuelsohn, Southwick, Corbin and Trafalgar. The Hound also features a full custom tailoring department for suits, sportcoats, slacks and shirts. Their knowledgeable staff will help with any of your clothing requirements.
Closed Sunday

ROCHESTER BIG & TALL CLOTHING
700 Mission St. at 3rd / 982-6455

As the premier fashion clothier for the man who is out of the ordinary in size and demands fashion with a sense of style, Rochester Big and Tall offers everything from suits to sportswear, tuxedos to shoes — in sizes 46 regular to 60 extra long. Designers include Perry Ellis, Charles Jourdan, Lanvin, Halston, Adolfo, Pierre Cardin, Ferrell Reed, Gant, Hathaway and Levi's. Shoes by Cole-Haan, Bally and Nike.
Open daily

ROYAL REGIMENT
San Francisco Shopping Centre / 227-0502

A resourceful Frenchman with an impeccable sense of style, Pierre Brouillet launched Royal Regiment to showcase his European designs. Brouillet travels the world to find the best fabrics and manufacturers for his classic line of shirts, slacks, sweaters, leather jackets, ties, belts and accessories.
Open daily

SAN FRANCISCO PENDLETON
464 Sutter St. at Powell / 788-6383

The famous Pendleton plaid shirts in soft virgin wool are plentiful here, but that's just the beginning. Men will love the selection of separates and sportswear.

SWAINE ADENEY
434 Post St. at Powell / 781-4949

Swaine Adeney features leather attaches and luggage, antique walking sticks, umbrellas, equestrian products and Barbour wax cotton outdoor wear.

DESIGNER WEAR FOR MEN

BARCELINO
498 Post St. at Mason / 781-5777

Recognized for its fine quality European men's apparel and elegant neo-Romanesque store interiors, Barcelino offers the finest collection of international men's wear in the Bay Area. The all-European clothing ranges from formal wear to business wear to sportswear, including a broad selection of designs by Belvest, Canali, Lubiam, Ravazzolo and others. Sophisticated, fashion-conscious men appreciate the clothing's natural fibers and classic, Continental styling. Other Barcelino locations include stores at the Fairmont and the Stouffer Stanford Court hotels in San Francisco, 819 Bridgeway in Sausalito, the Stanford Shopping Center in Palo Alto, the Valley Fair Mall in San Jose and the Sunvalley Mall in Concord.
Open daily & by appointment

COURTOUE
459 Geary St. at Taylor / 775-2900

Courtoue's collection of fine Italian clothing is one of the largest, with high-quality labels such as Brioni, Zegna and Canali. An excellent selection of Italian shoes finishes the look.

D. FINE
300 Post St. at Stockton / 986-3001

Some of the finest quality menswear made anywhere in the world is found at D. Fine. Featured are handmade

Michelangelo is featuring an exclusive collection of hand tailored clothing
and the latest fashion created by the the finest Italians Designers.
Our well trained staff will assist you with high quality merchandise
and first class service. We offer complimentary same
day alteration and delivery to your room.

"The Art of Men's Clothing"

355 Sutter Street. San Francisco, CA 94108 Tel.: 397-1447

suits and sports coats, shirts, leather jackets, ties and accessories in natural silks and cottons from Italy. Designers include Brioni, Canali, Jhane Barnes, Marol, New Man and Valentini.
Open daily

DAVID STEPHEN
117 Post St. at Kearny / 391-7710

You'll find classic Italian menswear here — suits, sports coats, slacks, sportswear and accessories — by Verri, Giorgio Armani, Versace Jeans Couture, Iceberg, Canali and Vestimenta.

DIAGONALE
352 Sutter St. at Grant / 397-3633

With an interior designed by one of Italy's foremost architects, and a staff chosen for its talent and experience, Diagonale is a boutique dedicated to bringing the best men's and women's European designer fashions to San Francisco. The collections carried reflect this ideal: Claude Montana, Thierry Mugler, Istante, Moschino, Iceberg and Jean Paul Gaultier, to name a few. Diagonale is located one block from Union Square.
Closed Sunday

EMPORIO ARMANI
One Grant Ave. at O'Farrell / 677-9400

The elegance of this historic building makes an ideal showcase for Giorgio Armani's designs. On the men's side, you'll find everything from suits and jackets to casual shirts and jeans. Beautiful ties, belts and shoes round out the collection.

GIANNI VERSACE FOR MEN
50 Post St., Crocker Galleria / 956-7957

Gianni Versace is known for his ability to blend cutting-edge fashion with beautiful fabrics, best exemplified by his contemporary designs for pants, jackets, coats and shoes. Classically cut and styled, with superb proportion and a touch of flamboyance, his line also includes suits, shirts, knitwear, hats, gloves, socks and accessories such as umbrellas and wallets. You'll find the complete collection in this elegant boutique.
Closed Sunday

MICHELANGELO
355 Sutter St. at Stockton / 397-1447

Experience the art in men's clothing. Michelangelo features an exclusive collection of handtailored clothing, as well as the latest fashions from Italy. The store has a good selection of suits and sportswear by Maurizio Baldassari, Nina Ricci, Nervesa and its own handtailored Michelangelo private label at very reasonable prices. The expert staff assists customers in making selections, and Michelangelo's first-class service includes complimentary same-day alteration and delivery to your hotel room.
Open daily

MIZANI UOMO
50 Post St., Crocker Galleria / 989-7900

Custom suiting at ready-made prices is the motto at Mizani, a "renaissance" menswear store packed with suits, sports coats and slacks in every style and weight. European-style shoes, belts, sweaters and shirts and a splendid array of bright neckties designed by Mizani inspire serious, one-stop shopping.
Closed Sunday

P. KELLER
San Francisco Shopping Centre / 974-6456

The award-winning interior of P. Keller offers an elegant and friendly setting for the man who appreciates contemporary yet sophisticated clothing. Since the suit is the backbone of its collections, P. Keller offers the best from Pal Zileri, Canali, Verri and Hugo Boss — plus a super selection of ties and dress shirts from Italy and Germany, and a presentation of unique European sportswear. Its knowledgeable sales staff awaits, eager to assist.
Open daily

POLO/RALPH LAUREN
90 Post St., Crocker Galleria / 567-POLO

A one-stop location in San Francisco for the entire family collection of famed American designer Ralph Lauren, this shop is an architectural testimony to elegance and refined taste. The multilevel interior features a collection of menswear, including activewear, classics, as well as accessories and footwear. Personalized service is a key asset of this must-see store, with a home furnishings department in the same location.
Closed Sunday

SULKA
255 Post St. at Stockton / 989-0600

Now in a spacious new store, the legendary Sulka maintains its tradition of superior shirts, ties and robes while adding a line of suits, shirts, ties, underwear and shoes.

SY AAL
1864 Union St. at Laguna / 929-1864

For Euro-American style clothing, men love Sy Aal on Union Street. Warm yet contemporary, her store will make them feel comfortable as they choose among the varied selection of unique shirts, jackets, slacks, ties, socks and belts, all in natural fabrics and subtle patterns. The American designers Sy Aal represents are top of the line, too, such as Jhane Barnes for great shirts and sweaters. "Frequent Tierrrz Club" members who receive her new ties by mail monthly agree with Sy — you can never have too many.
Open daily

VASARI
San Francisco Shopping Centre / 777-3501

A fresco ceiling, marble floors and Italian music create a stunning setting for Vasari's progressive designer wear — all individually selected in Europe for men and women.

VERSUS GIANNI VERSACE
50 Post St., Crocker Galleria / 616-0600

Renowned Italian designer Gianni Versace's long-awaited second line for men and women can be found in the new Versus boutique. It's a young, sexy collection, with Versace's trademark quality, fabric and workmanship but prices far below his couture collection. You'll find sportswear, leather, evening wear and an extensive line of accessories, from belts and ties to shoes and fragrance.
Closed Sunday

WILKES BASHFORD
375 Sutter St. at Stockton / 986-4380

Intimate merchandise groupings on five floors give Wilkes Bashford a feeling of great privilege and pampering. Among the designers carried are Issey Miyake, Thierry Mugler, Donna Karan, Brioni and Zegna.

MEN'S ACCESSORIES

FERRELL REED
161 Montgomery St. at Bush / 362-7717

Each tie is designed and colored by Ferrell Reed himself and handsewn from English and Italian silks, Scottish wools and Irish linens. The same quality can be found in the collection of 100 percent cotton shirts.

SKIVVIES
50 Post St., Crocker Galleria / 398-4886

Specializing in men's underwear, Skivvies stocks many European lines not found on the West Coast. Skivvies also showcases local designers of men's accessories.

MEN'S SHOES

ARTHUR BEREN SHOES
222 Stockton St. at Maiden Lane / 397-8900

With more than 40 years' experience, Arthur Beren Shoes selects only the finest footwear and accessories from designers and manufacturers from around the world. In the San Francisco spirit, the selection emphasizes superbly comfortable walking shoes and quietly elegant footwear for dress or business. Their spacious, two-level store offers a wide range of sizes, styles and colors for both men and women. Shoes by Salvatore Ferragamo, Cole-Haan, Mephisto and many others are featured, in a variety of styles that take you from daytime to evening,

SHOPPING

all through the week and into the weekend.
Open daily

AVVENTURA
San Francisco Shopping Centre / 546-1600

The man who cares about head-to-toe style will love Avventura's choice of dress and casual footwear, most created exclusively for the company in Italy. The line changes every season, guaranteeing fashion excitement.

BALLY OF SWITZERLAND
238 Stockton St. at Maiden Lane / 398-7463

Catering to an extremely refined clientele has earned Bally a reputation for having the highest quality shoes, handbags, luggage and leather accessories for men and women. Fine leather and suede clothing, attache cases, men's clutch bags and wallets round out the collection.
Open daily

BRUNO MAGLI
285 Geary St. at Powell / 421-0356

Bruno Magli's shoes for men are known the world over for comfort, quality and style. The store also features belts and leather jackets. Now you can find the entire European Salon collection in one place, Bruno Magli on Union Square.
Open daily

MARAOLO
404 Sutter St. at Stockton / 781-0895

Maraolo has made quality shoes for designers such as Armani in the Maraolo family factory. The San Francisco store also stocks handbags, belts, luggage and attaches.

RIA'S TIMBERLAND SHOP
900 North Point, Ghirardelli Square / 771-4393
437 Sutter St., Hyatt on Union Square / 398-0895

When only the real Timberland will do, those who know head for Ria's; the biggest selection of Timberland in Northern California is available here. The handsewn, waterproof leather shoes include moccasins, hiking and work boots, sandals, wingtips and bucks. You can also find wallets, belts, bags and other Timberland apparel and accessories. Ria carries more styles of Sebago loafers and Docksiders than anyone in the area. Also available are Sperry Topsiders, Bass, Birkenstocks, Ecco, Mephisto, Rockport, Clarks of England, Nike, Reeboks, the famous Alden shoe line from New England and authentic Western boots.
Open daily

22 STEPS
280 Sutter St. at Grant / 398-7797

In addition to cutting-edge women's shoes, 22 Steps features innovative European men's footwear by designers such as Paraboot, Dirk Bikkembergs and Luc Berjen.

WESTERN WEAR

EAST WEST LEATHER
1400 Grant Ave. at Green / 397-2886

East West offers western boots by Tony Lama and Justin, fashion leather garments for both men and women, and a range of accessories.

GROGERS WESTERN STORE
1445 Valencia St. btwn. 25th & 26th / 647-0700

With its vintage frontier cash register and desert cacti setting the mood for western wear purchases, Grogers attracts customers from all over the world.

WILD WILD WEST
838 Market St. at Powell / 986-7800
2193 Market St. at 15th / 626-1700

Wild Wild West has a complete selection of quality western clothing and gear.

CHILDREN'S STORES

BELLINI
418 Sutter St. at Stockton / 391-5417

With its complete selection of imported nursery furniture and top-quality accessories, Bellini is a godsend for the new parent, who will find everything from car seats, carriages, cribs and changing tables to infant clothing, gifts and toys in this two-story shop. Bellini has a registry for shower gifts and will ship anywhere in the world.
Open daily

CHARLOTTE'S WEB
2278 Union St. at Fillmore / 441-4700

Charlotte's Web has the best selection of children's books in the Bay Area. This friendly store carries books for children up to high-school age, videos, music and story tapes and guides for parents. Children who participate in the Birthday Club get a special discount during their birthday month. Charlotte's Web also sponsors author events, storytelling classes and discount programs for members of its Reader's Club.
Open daily

CITIKIDS BABY NEWS
1160 Post St. at Van Ness / 673-5437

A one-stop shop for major brand infant and toddler clothing, furniture, strollers, car seats, toys and every imaginable baby accessory.

DOTTIE DOOLITTLE
3680 Sacramento St. at Spruce / 563-3244

Dottie Doolittle offers an excellent selection of clothing and accessories for girls from infant to size 14 and for boys from infant to size 6X. The tailored classic styles are designed by Florence Eiseman, Jean Bourget, Cary and Mousefeathers. Dottie Doolittle has a new shoe store across the street, as well as a shop in Walnut Creek. *Open daily*

FAMILIAR, LTD.
1828 Union St. at Octavia / 563-0777

Founded in Japan by four women who saw a need for well-made children's clothing, Familiar, Ltd. opened its second U.S. store in San Francisco. The clothing for newborns to size 6 features the company's trademark bright plaids as well as Snoopy and Beatrix Potter storybook characters. All of the clothing is designed and manufactured in Japan, and the selection includes outstanding outfits for special occasions.
Open daily

FAO SCHWARZ
48 Stockton St. at O'Farrell / 394-8700

FAO Schwarz offers a wide selection of toys on three entertaining floors. An importer of Steiff and Trupa stuffed animals, FAO Schwarz also carries everything from crib toys to video games.

GROWING UP
240 West Portal Ave. at 14th Ave. / 661-6304

Growing Up has a full stock of infant and children's clothing, as well as unusual handmade items: dresses,

baby clothing, handknit sweaters and handpainted gifts. Growing Up's friendly owner will personalize your selection for your child.

IMAGINARIUM
3535 California St. at Laurel / 387-9885
Stonestown Galleria / 566-4111

The merchandise at Imaginarium is nonviolent, handpicked for quality, age-appropriateness and longevity, with a good balance of popular and specialty items.

KINDERSPORT JUNIOR SKI & SPORTS OUTFITTERS
3566 Sacramento St. at Laurel / 563-7778

KinderSport, America's original junior ski shop, specializes in the best ski clothing and equipment for children size 6 months to 16 years.

LES ENPHANTS
San Francisco Shopping Centre / 957-0588

"Let children be themselves" is the motto of Les Enphants, a private clothing label from Taiwan. You won't find pared-down adult styles, impractical designs or fussy patterns, only sturdy, natural fabrics cut in shapes that invite active play for children size infant to 8. Their children's shoe selection is one of the best in the city.
Open daily

SHOPPING

THE LITTLEST MOUSE
2550 California St. near Fillmore / 567-5121

Your child will be able to furnish the dollhouse of her dreams at The Littlest Mouse, a shop that specializes in dollhouses and dollhouse accessories.

QUINBY'S
3411 California St. at Laurel / 751-7727

What sets Quinby's apart is its unusual mix of books, tapes, videos and art supplies for ages 1 to 12 years. In one delightful trip, you can find a paperback on parenting, a set of sturdy playpen books, the latest Caldecott prize-winner, a fairy tale on tape, Babar's video adventures and new paints for your budding Picasso.
Open daily

TOYS 'R US
2675 Geary St. at Masonic / 931-8896
555 Ninth St. at Brannan / 252-0607

Toys 'R Us, the world's biggest toy store, is a pioneer in the specialty toy store business with more than 18,000 items in stock. You can get everything from diapers, formula, bikes and trains to clothing, planes and video games. The friendly sales staff helps answer questions and find gift items. Toys 'R Us has 16 other Bay Area locations.
Open daily

YOUNG MAN'S FANCY CLOTHIERS
3527 California St. at Laurel / 221-4230

Young Man's Fancy dresses boys from toddler-aged through the college years, and on into men's sizes.

YOUNTVILLE
2416 Fillmore St. at Jackson / 922-5050
Stonestown Galleria / 681-2202

The owners cater to infants, toddlers and children up to size 6X, emphasizing American, European and Japanese designers.
Open daily

BATH & PERFUME SHOPS

BARE ESCENTUALS
Embarcadero Center Three / 391-2830
2101 Chestnut St. at Steiner / 441-8348
Stonestown Galleria / 661-5255

For more than 16 years, Bare Escentuals has offered the highest quality all-natural color cosmetics and skin care products. The unique line of color contains no alcohol, perfume, talc, binders or fillers, all standard ingredients in most cosmetic products, which may irritate or damage the skin. Just as pure is the line of personal care products, including scented body lotions, aromatherapy products and fragrances for the home. Because Bare Escentuals is committed to protecting the environment, the products never contain animal ingredients, nor are they tested on animals. All packaging is 100 percent recyclable, and cus-

tomers who return used bottles for refills are rewarded with special discounts.
Open daily

CRABTREE & EVELYN
50 Post St., Crocker Galleria / 392-6111

Crabtree & Evelyn's reputation for fine quality toiletries is unsurpassed. Other stores are at Ghirardelli Square and Embarcadero One.

THE HERBALIST BATH & BODY SHOP
3610A Sacramento St. at Locust / 771-8330

The finest European lines of bath and body products are available in this fragrant boutique, including L'Herbier de Provence from France, Floris of London and Bronnley of London, an outstanding selection of perfumes for men and women. You'll also find aromatherapy as well as massage oils and essential oils, back brushes, loofahs, towels, soaps, bath essences, wreaths, topiaries, potpourri, dried flowers, wall hangings and other unique gifts. The Herbalist is a one-stop shop for pampering yourself and those you love.
Open daily

GIFTS

AERIAL
2801 Leavenworth St., The Cannery / 474-1566

You'll find architectural books and prints, goggles, whistles, Mitre soccer balls, sports clothing and accessories, leather jackets, jewelry and fine-art supplies.

BORETTI
900 North Point, Ghirardelli Square / 928-3340

The owner is a specialist in Baltic Sea amber, and several museum-quality pieces are on display in her impressive collection. Folk art is also available.

DUDLEY PERKINS COMPANY
66 Page St. at Market / 703-9477

Established in 1914, Dudley Perkins Company is the oldest Harley-Davidson store in existence, run by the same family of enthusiasts since it opened. In addition to motorcycles and Harley-Davidson's great line of clothing, Dudley Perkins stocks all the accessories and collectibles: pocket knives, scarves, T-shirts, belts, hats, key chains, gloves, wallets, pens, lighters, etc... Distinguished by the famous Harley-Davidson logo, they make memorable gifts or souvenirs. While you're there, spend some time admiring the collection of vintage motorcycles.
Closed Sunday

FLAX ART & DESIGN
1699 Market St. at Valencia / 552-2355

San Francisco's leading supply store for artists since 1938, Flax recently expanded to an award-winning

20,000-square-foot showplace for original gifts, frames, stationery, fine pens and, of course, artists' materials. Flax's world-famous paper department boasts thousands of sheets for every use. The store offers a marvelous environment for creative people, and there is plenty of free parking to make your visit even easier.
Closed Sunday

GOOSEBUMPS
900 North Point, Ghirardelli Square / 928-2112

Goosebumps has a variety of gifts — from gag items to cards, T-shirts and the largest selection of upscale earrings in the city.

THE NATURE COMPANY
Embarcadero Four, street level / 956-4911
900 North Point, Ghirardelli Square / 776-0724

A Bay Area tradition since 1972, this complete specialty retailer of the natural world has outdoor discovery tools for all ages, natural history books, binoculars, nature prints and posters, and other nature-related items.

OUR LITTLE HOUSE
2800 Leavenworth St., The Anchorage / 776-1871

Almost everything here is handcrafted in the United States and personally selected by the owners. You'll find potpourri, folk dolls, door harps and a variety of gifts.

THE SHARPER IMAGE
532 Market St. at Sutter / 398-6472
900 North Point, Ghirardelli Square / 776-1443

The Sharper Image develops, introduces and sells a unique assortment of original gifts. The two San Francisco stores display today's most innovative executive toys. Aficionados of high tech will enjoy the state-of-the-art instruments and unusual gifts, all personally tested and quality-approved by the originator of the outlet. The Sharper Image's collection of high-tech, electronics, health, fitness, home furnishing, recreational and novelty items is also available by mail order from a colorful monthly catalog.
Open daily

MAPS & GUIDES

THOMAS BROS. MAPS & BOOKS
550 Jackson St. at Columbus / 981-7520

Lost? Thomas Bros. carries a full assortment of maps, guides, atlases, travel books and a large selection of globes to help you find your way. In the same building since 1960, the store is furnished with handmade drawers overflowing with every kind of map imaginable. There are giant wall maps, laminated maps, hanging maps, maps of the stars, ocean floors and of every country, state, city and nook and cranny in the world. Thomas Bros. offers demographic maps and special guides geared for the business traveler.
Closed Saturday & Sunday

SHOPPING

Thank you: Wilkes Bashford; Andy Marshall, Jennifer Wolf, EPIC Models

a high quality of life. San Francisco style is fresh, personal and sophisticated. It shows off in an intelligent way, playful yet elegant. Here, as elsewhere, economy and concern for the environment motivate the design trends of the decade: freedom of personal expression, global eclecticism, artistic spirit, comfort and value.

Introduced by Agnes Bourne

Agnes Bourne owns Agnes Bourne Studio in San Francisco, which represents Artfurniture and complementary lines and fabrics. Ms. Bourne also designs furniture and interiors.

Even if you have only a little money, you can still change the feel of your home. The easiest way is to change the color of the walls and ceilings. Shifting the furniture from the conventional square arrangement to a floating diagonal can enliven your living space, transforming it from the usual squared-off arrangement.

To add a sense of joy and fun, choose pieces that have histories or tell stories. Mix with utilitarian antiques, old woods and metals, fresh plaids and tickings. Not funky, but ironic objects work best, like iron flowers, leather and feathers, mohair and silk — anything that has the spirit of the maker and the sense of being handmade.

Feeling good. Being free. Having fun. Celebrating yourself. Working well. When they come together, your world supports you at being your best, in harmony with the environment you create. As you spruce up your home, you create well-being. Your heart sings; your mind sparkles with new ideas; your body sighs with comfort — all because your eyes tell you the world is beautiful.

THE WAVE MOVES FORWARD

The Beosystem® 2500 is an advancement in audio systems
beyond anything you've seen or heard before.

Its inventive design actually makes the sound waves behave
as if they are originating from a much larger system.
Ingeniously, it is both a thing of beauty and an object of great intelligence.

Witness how the Beosystem 2500 involves all of your senses. Extend your hand to the front of the
system and see how the glass doors slide open and the light comes on, as if by magic.

In six decorator colors, it is an entirely new look in audio systems.

Experience Bang & Olufsen and discover the incredible sound of the Beosystem 2500.
It makes waves like they've never been made before.

Purveyor to H.M. The Queen of Denmark
Est. 1925

Bang & Olufsen®
San Francisco
345 Powell Street, Union Square   (415) 274-3320

CRYSTAL, CHINA & SILVER

THE ENCHANTED CRYSTAL
1771 Union St. at Gough / 885-1335

The fantasy window created by The Enchanted Crystal each month is in itself worth the trip to Union Street. But step inside and discover why it is acclaimed as one of San Francisco's most magical places to shop. This store specializes in art glass, decorative crystal and jewelry in crystal and glass.
Open daily

GLASS PHEASANT
239 Grant Ave. at Post / 391-8377

Glass Pheasant displays fine crystal and art glass from all over the world, with many unique styles and shapes of one-of-a-kind items. Don't miss the collectible gallery of famous porcelain figurines, crystal engraved objets d'art and decorator pieces for the home. Glass Pheasant's fine jewelry department has treasures from the real to the faux, including designer pins, necklaces and rings. With its impeccable service and beautiful selection, Glass Pheasant is a memorable store you'll want to visit again and again.
Closed Sunday

GUMP'S
250 Post St. at Grant / 982-1616

Gump's has the largest choice of European porcelain and bone china in San Francisco, as well as the widest collection of Baccarat crystal and fine French silver in the United States.

PAUL BAUER
156 Geary St. at Grant / 421-6862

Known for European china and crystal, Paul Bauer carries hand-painted porcelains, crystal and figurines, including a huge collection of Lladro from Spain.

PAVILLON CHRISTOFLE
140 Grant Ave. at Maiden Lane / 399-1931

Pavillon Christofle carries exquisite sterling silver, gold-plated and stainless steel flatware. You'll also find 18-karat gold jewelry and elegant gift items.

WATERFORD WEDGWOOD
304 Stockton St. at Post / 391-5610

Waterford Wedgwood has an extensive variety of tableware and crystal that is sure to match your needs.

LINENS

KRIS KELLY
One Union Square, 174 Geary St. / 986-8822

Whether your taste runs to pristine or frilly, you'll love Kris Kelly's exclusive collection of bed and table linens embellished with embroidery or handmade lace.

SCHEUER LINENS
318 Stockton St. at Post / 392-2813

For three generations the Scheuer family has offered the finest linens. Their tablecloth and placemat selection includes Madeira handwork, damask linen and Belgian prints. For the bedroom, there are 100 percent cotton sheets imported from Europe as well as high-quality comforters, bedspreads and duvet covers with matching accessories. Monogrammed towels for the bath are also a specialty.
Closed Sunday

SUE FISHER KING
3067 Sacramento St. at Baker / 922-7276

This charming store carries exclusive linen imports as well as robes and gowns, European toiletries and Italian pottery for the tabletop.

HOUSEWARES & HOME ACCESSORIES

ARTIFACTS
3024 Fillmore St. near Union / 922-8465

One of the most inviting stores in San Francisco, Artifacts offers an ever-changing array of affordable fine art, contemporary craft and interior accessories, all beautifully displayed in the gallery. This is the perfect place for gifts or a little self-indulgence. Objects may be functional or decorative, but the pieces are always carefully selected for design, quality and originality. Artifacts is also well known for its excellent selection of jewelry. The friendly, service-oriented store offers shipping and complimentary gift wrapping and welcomes special requests. There is also a corporate gift service.
Open daily

INTERIORS

ASHLING
517 Sutter St. at Powell / 986-8663

A beautiful new store near Union Square, Ashling is the place to go for traditional and contemporary home accessories, including many handcrafted pieces. You'll find gift items and toys in addition to candlesticks, linens, cushions, china, crystal, frames, soaps and much more. Ashling has something unique in every price range.
Closed Sunday

COTTONWOOD
3461 Sacramento St. at Walnut / 346-6020

Chosen for their elegant yet primitive appeal, the contemporary handcrafted furniture and home accessories at Cottonwood combine beauty, function and a Southwestern feel.

CRATE AND BARREL
125 Grant Ave. at Maiden Lane / 986-4000

Crate and Barrel is chock-full of housewares priced to please any budget, from glasses and dishes to cutlery, pots, pans and gourmet items.

FILLAMENTO
2185 Fillmore St. at Sacramento / 931-2224

If expressing contemporary, personal style is a must, Fillamento has everything needed to create a signature environment for the nineties. The store offers creative decorating choices for every room of your home. An ever-changing selection of home furnishings, accessories, dinnerware and tabletop collections ranges from formal to casual, and an expert staff provides intelligent advice, shipping and delivery services, and free gift wrapping.
Open daily

GRIFFIN NEEDLEPOINT BOUTIQUE
344 Presidio Ave. at Sacramento / 567-1712

Located within Heart of the Lion, this is the place to go for everything you need to do beautiful needlepoint. You'll find miniature French arm chairs in muslin with a variety of needlepoint canvas designs by owner Martha Rosen. Also featured are antique needlepoint pieces, Paternayan, Medici and specialty fibers, as well as a large selection of tassels, trims and French ribbons. Blocking and finishing services are also offered.
Closed Sunday

IT'S MY HOUSE
1905 Fillmore St. at Pine / 346-8000

This lovely new store is a one-stop shop not only for home accessories and furniture, but also for custom sewing to personalize any room in your home. Window treatments come in many styles with a wide choice of fabrics, and upholstery and seat and sofa covers are a specialty. You'll also find chairs, sofas and ottomans made

to order and sturdy recycled and new pine furniture.
Open daily

LA VILLE DU SOLEIL
444 Post St. at Mason / 434-0657

Almost everything is French in this beautiful downtown store, from the pillows, shams and tabletop linens to the handpainted dishes. A few French antiques are also available.

PIERRE DEUX
120 Maiden Lane at Grant / 296-9940

These 100 percent cotton prints from the south of France continue a tradition established 300 years ago. People who really know fabric admire the floral designs for their color and depth of hues, and for the decidedly French provincial look of the prints. Pierre Deux also offers authentic French Country furnishings from the different provinces of France, ranging from French antique and reproduction furniture to tableware, custom table and bed linens, home fragrances and pewterware.
Closed Sunday

POLO/RALPH LAUREN
90 Post St. at Kearny, Crocker Galleria / 567-POLO

Ralph Lauren's home collection is presented in complete room groupings that show the trademark Lauren look to full advantage. Bed linens, towels, bath accessories, wallpaper, rugs, pillows, fabrics and blankets set off Lauren's wicker beds and upholstered furniture. The store also features exquisite fine china and crystal.
Closed Sunday

POTTERY BARN
2000 Chestnut St. at Fillmore / 441-1787

Pottery Barn carries contemporary, well-crafted and affordable home accessories, including candlesticks, vases and table settings, as well as handsome kitchen tables and chairs. You'll also find Pottery Barn in Embarcadero One and Stonestown Galleria.

RH
2506 Sacramento St. at Fillmore / 346-1460

A charming house and garden accessories resource, RH carries potted plants, table tops from Italy and Portugal and wire work — including baskets, planters, candlesticks and wreaths — by local artists. Patio furniture comes in classic wicker, hand-finished metal by Winterther and even cast concrete.
Open daily

VIGNETTE
3625 Sacramento St. at Locust / 567-0174

Vignette's eclectic collection of home and personal accessories is marked by the artistic touch of its owner. Lynn Getz chooses unusual items from here and abroad

INTERIORS

and presents them in beautiful vignettes. You'll find handsome frames, handmade linens, one-of-a-kind bowls and dishes, wood and metal candlesticks, small tables, lamps, clocks — in short, just the object to pull a room together with unmistakable style.
Closed Sunday

WILKESHOME
375 Sutter St. at Stockton / 986-4380

In addition to designer wear, Wilkes Bashford carries home accessories and gifts in its newly added home furnishings department.

WILLIAMS-SONOMA
150 Post St. at Grant / 362-6904

Williams-Sonoma provides the finest kitchenware, housewares and specialty foods. Other stores are in Embarcadero Two, San Francisco Shopping Centre and Stonestown Galleria.

Z GALLERIE
2071 Union St. at Webster / 346-9000

Z Gallerie has original designs in furniture, lighting, accessories and posters. Z Gallerie is also in the San Francisco Shopping Centre, Stonestown Galleria and at 1465 Haight Street.

DESIGN CONSULTANTS

BUY DESIGN
2 Henry Adams St., Showplace Design Ctr. / 626-4944

Buy Design provides access to Showplace Square Design Center's 350 wholesale furniture, fabric, floorcovering and lighting showrooms without an interior decorator.

ROOM BY ROOM DESIGN
2 Henry Adams St., Showplace Design Ctr. / 621-8722

Room By Room's interior design team helps clients plan all elements of their living spaces, then recommends showrooms, stores and subcontractors to carry out the plan.

FOLK ART & CRAFT GALLERIES

FOLK ART INTERNATIONAL & XANADU GALLERY
900 North Point, Ghirardelli Square / 441-5211

Ancient and contemporary folk art from West Africa, Mexico, Central America, Indonesia, India and the Philippines fills two spacious rooms with a captivating variety of objects.

GHIRARDELLI CRAFT GALLERY
900 North Point, Ghirardelli Square / 441-0780

Specializing in West Coast artists, the gallery offers

handcrafted wood boxes and baskets, handpainted tiles, pottery, earrings and jewelry.

IMAGES OF THE NORTH
1782 Union St. at Octavia / 673-1273

Located in one of Union Street's charming Victorians, Images of the North features an extensive collection of museum-quality Inuit (Eskimo) sculpture. The collection also includes Inuit and Northwest Coast prints and masks. Exhibitions are presented throughout the year, highlighting individual artists, themes and communities (including the Cape Dorset prints).
Open daily

JAPONESQUE
824 Montgomery St. at Jackson / 398-8577

Koichi Hara has assembled a beautiful array of museum-quality Japanese art, which draws collectors from all over the world. Each of the unique pieces of sculpture, pottery or glass, many of them rare to California, is introduced and explained by Mr. Hara.
Closed Sunday

SMILE
500 Sutter St. at Powell / 362-3436

Known as the gallery with "tongue in chic," Smile is dedicated to the glory of the imagination. An eclectic array of folk art, sculpture, paintings, furniture and one-of-a-kind clothing and jewelry represents more than 100 mostly Bay Area artists. Art experts, neophytes and fun seekers alike will definitely smile at this unusual, affordable collection, teasing to be given as gifts or to be taken home.
Closed Sunday

VIRGINIA BREIER
3091 Sacramento St. at Baker / 929-7173

Everything carried by Virginia Breier is crafted by hand in America, from outstanding earrings and colorful pottery to sculptures, mirrors, chairs and chests.

HOME ELECTRONICS

AUDIO EXCELLENCE
528 Washington St. at Sansome / 433-1335

Audio Excellence features a full range of sound equipment for the stereo enthusiast.

BANG & OLUFSEN SAN FRANCISCO
345 Powell St. at Post, Union Square / 274-3320

Bang & Olufsen audio and video systems each have their own individual personalities, encompassing advanced technology, ease of operation and beautiful Danish design. No less than 16 products have found their way into the permanent collection of the Museum of Modern Art in New York. Customers can explore a new world of vision and sound possibility with Bang & Olufsen's custom-designed home electronics, which the staff will expertly install.
Closed Sunday

HOUSE OF MUSIC
2 Bryant St. at Embarcadero / 243-9888

House of Music represents many of the finest names in the audio industry and provides home installation and maintenance service.

PERFORMANCE AUDIO
2847 California St. at Divisadero / 441-6220
816 Mission St. at 4th / 543-4507

Listen and view equipment in multiple "home-style" environments, then get free delivery and professional installation.

STEREO PLUS
2201 Market St. at Sanchez / 861-1044

The finest names in audio and home theatre can be found at Stereo Plus — B&W, Krell, Apogee, Adcom, Pro-Ac, Mirage, Conrad-Johnson, PS Audio and many other brands of high-performance equipment. All are backed by an exclusive double warranty, with factory service, custom design and installation, and expert advice by a staff with decades of experience. Free parking.
Open daily

WORLD OF SOUND
1900 Van Ness Ave. at Washington / 928-3101

In business since 1966, World of Sound offers an excellent selection of audio and video high-fidelity components and operates the largest independently owned service center in Northern California. World of Sound sells audio equipment by ADS, Bang & Olufsen, Kef, Luxman, Monitor Audio, Mitsubishi, Nakamichi, McIntosh, Phase Technology and many others, all backed by a double warranty at no extra charge. You'll also find CWD modular cabinetry to store all your equipment in style. Free parking.
Open daily

RUGS

CARPETS OF THE INNER CIRCLE
444 Jackson St. at Montgomery / 398-2988

One of the finest collections of large and oversized decorative carpets on the West Coast can be found at Carpets of the Inner Circle.

JALILI INTERNATIONAL
235 Kansas St., Showplace Sq. South / 788-3377

A purveyor of high-quality Oriental rugs since 1880, Jalili offers antique and contemporary rugs from Persia, India, Pakistan, China, Turkey, Romania and Afghanistan.

INTERIORS

ROCHE-BOBOIS
CENTER STAGE

Much like a great actor, a Roche-Bobois sofa plays with light and space to its very best advantage. It always wins the leading role in your room, offering command performances in both classic and contemporary settings.

FRAME SHOPS

Got a few posters you've been meaning to frame? Can't figure out how to display that photo taken in Europe? Here are some places that can do it in style.

CITY PICTURE FRAME
520 3rd St. at Bryant / 543-4105

Provides museum-quality frames and mats. Large selection and reliable service. By appointment only.
Closed Sunday

FAULKNER CUSTOM FRAMING
1200 Folsom St. at 8th / 861-2800

A division of Faulkner Color Labs, this is the place to go for quality, innovative photo mounting. The store also offers 11 years of experience mounting three-dimensional and oversized objects.
Closed Sunday

FLAX
1699 Market St. at Valencia / 552-2355

San Francisco's leading supply store for artists since 1938, Flax also does custom framing. Free quotes, competitive pricing and more than 500 styles of molding are just a few of Flax's charms. Expanded to a 20,000-square-foot showplace, Flax also offers original gifts, stationery, fine pens, artists' materials and an outstanding paper department, boasting thousands of sheets for every use. Plenty of free parking available.
Closed Sunday

KIMURA FRAMING & GALLERY INC.
1933 Ocean Ave. at Keystone / 585-0052

Family owned for more than 30 years, this full-service framer handles needlework, Oriental art and unusual objects. Most jobs are completed in one week.
Closed Sunday, Monday & Thursday

PACIFIC FRAMING COMPANY
1640 Union St. at Franklin / 673-7263

More than 4,000 styles of molding are available here, with an emphasis on preservation and conservation framing. Specialties: fabric wraps and gold-leaf bevels.
Open daily

UNIQUE CUSTOM FRAMERS & GALLERY
4129 18th St. at Castro / 431-2333

Creators of inlaid mats, Unique Custom Framers stresses conservation work and provides frames for many city galleries.
Open daily

RETURN TO TRADITION
3315 Sacramento St. at Presidio / 921-4180

The exclusive dealer for DOBAG carpets in the United States, Return to Tradition sells hand-knotted carpets from 40 mountain villages in western Turkey, where Anatolian weavers recreate stunning geometric designs handed down through the centuries.

SORAYA ORIENTAL RUGS
2 Henry Adams St., Showplace Design Ctr. / 626-5757

Accolades from interior designers and their clientele have earned Soraya a reputation for its magnificent collection of more than 5,000 new and antique rugs.

FURNITURE

CONCEPTS
398 Kansas St. at 17th / 864-7776

Just a block from Showplace Square, Concepts is a spacious, well-designed store for furniture previously available only through an interior decorator.

DAK SAN FRANCISCO
444 DeHaro St. at 17th / 558-9144

High-quality modular furniture for home and office is designed and installed by a friendly team of trained DAK professionals.

GALISTEO
590 10th St. at Division / 861-5900

Galisteo's bright, huge showroom is packed with colorful, earthy furniture, crafts and home accessories from the Southwest, including antiques and made-to-order pieces, all available directly to the public. Just steps away from Showplace Square, this is the largest Southwestern collection on the West Coast. The store also features antique and early California furniture, custom cabinets and armoires, primitive furniture, folk art, Western and cowboy memorabilia, rugs, blankets and custom-upholstered sofas and chairs.
Open daily

ICF
550 Pacific Ave. at Montgomery / 433-3231

For more than 30 years, ICF has been bringing the finest international furniture collections to America. Represented are the world's greatest architects and designers in an assemblage of chairs, desks, tables and lounge seating for both the home and office. Among the featured designers are the renowned Josef Hoffmann, Alvar Aalto, Arne Jacobsen and Richard Neutra and such new American talents as Bob Josten and Tod Williams. Many of the showcased pieces are part of permanent museum collections.
Closed Sunday

JUVENILE LIFESTYLES, INC.
541 Eighth St. at Bryant / 863-4411

The only designer showroom exclusively dedicated to children's rooms, Juvenile Lifestyles makes fantasies come true with their selection of more than 95 lines.

LIMN COMPANY
290 Townsend St. at 4th / 543-5466

At the cutting edge of furniture design worldwide, Limn is full of fresh, exciting, often experimental new pieces. Located in its enormous new building South of Market, the store features products from Europe, America and Asia — more than 500 lines of modern design.
Closed Sunday

LIMN COMPANY PACIFIC
457 Pacific Ave. at Sansome / 397-7474

A new design store selling the work of California artisans and other well-known American designers, Limn offers unusual ready-to-purchase furniture, lamps and accessories as well as complete custom design services.
Closed Sunday

NEXT INTERIORS
50 Van Ness Ave. at Fell / 255-7662

Next offers furniture and lighting for every room, dis-played in elegant groupings that will make it easy for you to visualize the sleek pieces in your own home.

POSTMARK
445A Sutter St. at Stockton / 788-7678

Carrying a wide range of medium to high-end Italian furniture, Postmark offers classics, contemporary soft goods with exciting fabrics and leathers, 100 percent wool area rugs and the latest in contemporary furniture from Milan. The store also represents German lighting designer Ingo Maurer's line.
Closed Sunday & Monday

ROCHE BOBOIS
One Henry Adams St. at Kansas / 626-8613

Roche Bobois specializes in the import of an exclusive collection of designer furniture and accessories for residential and executive office design. Recognized as the world leader in contemporary European furniture, Roche Bobois offers two exciting and distinct collections: Les Nouveaux Classiques, featuring a line of classic contemporary furniture, and Les Provinciales, a collection of beautifully handcrafted French period furniture in solid cherry, walnut and other fine fruit woods.
Closed Sunday

INTERIORS

TECHLINE STUDIO
680 8th St., Sobel Bldg., Suite 163 / 431-7710

The premier line in modular laminate furniture, Techline is affordable, flexible and aesthetically pleasing.

ZINC DETAILS
906 Post St. at Hyde / 346-1422

Zinc Details is an innovative retail and wholesale studio representing a wide range of Bay Area and national talent with functional, affordable furniture and accessories for the contemporary home and office. Focusing on new designers and architects, Zinc Details exhibits everything from versatile chairs, stools and tables to original light fixtures and such home accents as frames, baskets and vases. The sunny storefront on the flanks of San Francisco's Nob Hill is five blocks west of Union Square.
Open daily

ANTIQUES

ANTONIO'S ANTIQUES
701 Bryant St. at 5th / 781-1737
701 Sansome St. at Jackson / 781-1737

The largest antique showroom on the West Coast, Antonio's on Bryant features English and Continental furniture and accessories of the 17th, 18th and early 19th centuries. An authority in restoration, Antonio's has brought priceless pieces back to their original splendor for museums and collectors.
Closed Sunday

ASHKENAZIE & CO.
Fairmont Hotel
950 Mason St. at California / 391-3440

The largest collection of antique Chinese jade works of art in the world can be found at Ashkenazie. They also carry Japanese *netsuke* and art works.

CHALLISS HOUSE
463 Jackson St. at Sansome / 397-6999
2 Henry Adams St., Showplace Design Ctr. / 863-1566

Challiss House offers fine English and Continental furniture, Tiffany lamps, sculpture and porcelains.

CLAIRE THOMSON ANTIQUES
495 Jackson St. near Montgomery / 986-4453

Claire Thomson Antiques features 18th and 19th century English furniture and accessories, specializing in porcelains, ironstone and Staffordshire figure groups.

DANIEL STEIN ANTIQUES
458 Jackson St. at Sansome / 956-5620

Specializing in 18th and 19th century English and American furniture and accessories, Daniel Stein Antiques is known for its collection of brass telescopes.

DILLINGHAM & COMPANY
470 Jackson St. at Montgomery / 989-8777

This gracious showroom specializes in collector-quality English antiques from 1650-1820, and emphasizes the fine original condition and distinction of the pieces.

DRUM & COMPANY
415 Jackson St. at Sansome / 788-5118

This sophisticated store offers 17th, 18th and early 19th century English and Continental furniture as well as porcelain, paintings, lamps and unusual accessories.

ED HARDY/SAN FRANCISCO
750 Post St. at Jones / 771-6644

Ed Hardy's collection of 17th and 18th century Oriental and European antiques includes Japanese screens, French gilt-wood consoles, Ming lacquers and English mahogany and walnut furniture.

EVELYN'S ANTIQUE CHINESE FURNITURE INC.
381 Hayes St. at Gough / 255-1815

Evelyn's is one of the best resources for antique 17th to 19th century Chinese furniture and accessories.

EVELYNE CONQUARET ANTIQUES
550 15th St., Showplace Square West / 552-6100

In this showroom you will find 18th and 19th century French antiques, including a wide selection of tables, desks, buffets, dressers and armoires, exclusively chosen by the owner.

FOSTER-GWIN ANTIQUES
425 Jackson St. at Montgomery / 397-4986

Specializing in 17th, 18th and 19th century English and Continental furniture and decorations, Foster-Gwin has established a reputation for handsome collectible items.

FUMIKI FINE ASIAN ARTS
2001 Union St. at Buchanan / 922-0573

Fumiki Fine Arts displays the works, old and new, of artists and artisans from throughout the Orient. Exhibited on two floors, the collection includes Japanese antique baskets, imari, tansu and the Bay Area's best selection of obis (used for table runners and wall hangings), Korean chests and celadon. The store's extensive selection of wooden stands is perfect for presenting Fumiki's fine porcelains.
Open daily

GENJI
1731 Buchanan St. at Post / 931-1616

Genji has been importing beautiful and traditional Japanese antiques to the Bay Area since 1974. Today, the store is known as the best source for antique Japanese furniture, kimonos, obis and folk arts. At Genji, you'll find excellent antiques at affordable prices.
Open daily

HAWLEY BRAGG
3364 Sacramento St. at Presidio / 563-8122

Hawley Bragg carries a diverse collection of 18th and 19th century Continental furnishings and decorative accessories.

HEART OF THE LION
344 Presidio Ave. at Sacramento / 567-1712

This chic Presidio Heights shop specializes in Biedermeier and French Empire antiques. Spotted cats and lions abound, in porcelain and bronze as well as prints and drawings. Also featured are pillows made from antique fabric fragments. Griffin Needlepoint Boutique is located within the shop, offering custom canvas designs by owner Martha Rosen.
Closed Sunday

HIGHGATE ANTIQUES
441 Jackson St. at Montgomery / 397-0800

A huge shop on Jackson Square, Highgate features a full range of Oriental art as well as a large selection of Persian rugs and 18th and 19th century English and Continental antiques.

HUNT ANTIQUES
478 Jackson St. at Montgomery / 989-9531

Brian Hunt carries a wonderful selection of 17th to 19th century country and formal furniture from England and the Continent.

JOHN DOUGHTY ANTIQUES
619 Sansome St. at Jackson / 398-6849

John and Wendy Doughty have visited their native England every 12 weeks for the last 20 years to keep their large Jackson Square showroom full of superior quality 18th and 19th century English furniture, paintings and a huge range of accessories. This warm, friendly showroom is a *must* for all antique lovers.
Closed Saturday & Sunday

KUROMATSU
722 Bay St. at Leavenworth / 474-4027

The emphasis at Kuromatsu is on Japanese country-style or "Mingei" artifacts, personally selected in Japan by John Cook. Established in 1962, the gallery specializes in ikebana baskets, tansu, ceramics and decorative accessories.
Closed Sunday

LES POISSON
3489 Sacramento St. at Laurel / 441-7537

A beautiful arrangement of Country French antiques and 19th Century paintings fills this store. A direct importer who travels to France twice a year, the owner is infatuated with the art and history of the pieces he

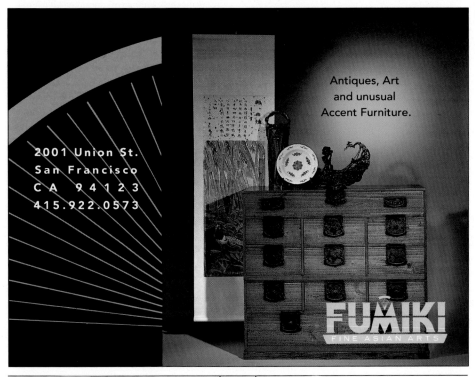
INTERIORS

discovers, and his passion is contagious. A complete decorating service and a French architectural consultant are available to help customers. If you're down in Los Gatos, make sure to visit Les Poisson's new store at 25 North Santa Cruz Avenue (408-354-7937).
Closed Sunday

MARCELINE BURRELL, INC.
412 Jackson St. at Sansome / 986-0823

This delightful antiques gallery offers major collections of 18th century Continental furniture, works of art, custom-made lamps and decorative accessories.

ORIENTATIONS
34 Maiden Lane at Grant / 981-3972

Orientations presents individually chosen Oriental antiques, furniture, paintings and porcelains. The history of various pieces and, in some cases, the exact point of origin are described by a well-informed and attentive staff.
Closed Sunday

ROBERT DOMERGUE & COMPANY
560 Jackson St. at Columbus / 781-4034

Robert Domergue & Company specializes in fine 17th and 18th century Continental furniture. While the focus is mainly on French decorative arts of the 18th century, painted furniture from Italy and other parts of Europe is offered. Early 19th century scenic wallpapers are also of interest.
Closed Saturday & Sunday

ROBERT HERING AND ASSOCIATES
3307 Sacramento St. at Presidio / 563-4144

Robert Hering offers 18th and 19th century English and Continental antiques, accessories and lamps as well as traditional upholstery services.

THERIEN & COMPANY
411 Vermont St. at 17th / 956-8850

The finest selections of 17th and 18th century furniture, Oriental carpets and rugs, Old Sheffield plates and porcelain are displayed at Therien & Company.

THOMAS LIVINGSTON ANTIQUES
455 Jackson St. at Sansome / 296-8150

For fine English and American furniture from the late 18th and early 19th century, visit Thomas Livingston Antiques on Jackson Square.

T.Z. SHIOTA
3131 Fillmore St. at Greenwich / 929-7979

In a bright corner location at Pixley Lane, T.Z. Shiota provides a tranquil setting for exquisite Japanese art, beautifully displayed.

WALKER MCINTYRE ANTIQUES
3419 Sacramento St. at Walnut / 563-8024

On Sacramento Street for 16 years, Walker McIntyre features a large collection of 18th and 19th century fine English and Continental furniture. The store specializes in Georgian mahogany dining room pieces and chairs. Walker McIntyre also has one of the best collections of antique porcelain on the West Coast, including large selections of 19th century Imari, Rose Medallion and English porcelain.
Closed Sunday

GALLERIES

THE ALLRICH GALLERY
251 Post St. at Stockton / 398-8896

The Allrich Gallery is known for its support of the fiber arts. Noted artists include Nance O'Banion, Olga de Amaral, Lia Cook, Jerry Concha and Dan Snyder.

BOWLES-SOROKKO GALLERIES
765 Beach St. btwn. Larkin & Hyde / 441-8008

The gallery carries original paintings, etchings, serigraphs and lithographs by Leroy Neiman and Mihail Chemiakin, along with sculptures by Bay Area artist Paul Braslow.

BRAUNSTEIN/QUAY GALLERY
250 Sutter St. at Grant / 392-5532

This contemporary gallery displays sculpture, paintings and drawings by leading artists, including John Altoon, Peter Voulkos, Jeremy Anderson and Mary Snowden.

CAMPBELL-THIEBAUD GALLERY
647 Chestnut St. at Columbus / 441-8680

This intimate artspace is devoted mostly to figurative and landscape artists of the Bay Area, including Lundy Siegriest, Charles Griffin Farr and Wayne Thiebaud.

CIRCLE GALLERY
140 Maiden Lane at Stockton / 989-2100

Designed by Frank Lloyd Wright, this beautiful building is a perfect backdrop for fine art jewelry by Braque, Cocteau, Erte and others, in addition to graphic works and sculpture.

COBRA FINE ART
580 Sutter St. at Mason / 397-2195

Named after a European art movement of the late 1940s and early '50s, Cobra Fine Art has assembled an impressive collection of contemporary work by artists of international renown. For a look at what's happening in fine art around the world without leaving San Francisco, this is the place to go. Among those represented are Rudi Pillen (Belgium), Sven Inge (Sweden), Victor Chab (Argentina), Edo Murtic (Croatia), Andras Markos (Germany), Alain Grosajt (France), Antoni Tapies (Spain), Fons Bloemen (Holland) and Paula Townsend (U.S.).
Open daily & Sunday by appointment

CONACHER GALLERIES
134 Maiden Lane at Stockton / 392-5447

Conacher features internationally known contemporary realists, including Peter Ellenshaw, Eyvind Earle, Elizabeth Charleston, Merv Corning and Alan Maley.

CONTEMPORARY REALIST GALLERY
23 Grant Ave. at O'Farrell, 6th floor / 362-7152

Contemporary Realist specializes in representational paintings by American artists such as Willard Dixon, Gabriel Laderman and Jane Fisher.

DON SOKER GALLERY
251 Post St. at Stockton / 291-0966

This gallery specializes in innovative works by leading Japanese and Bay Area artists, including T.V. Jones, Kenjilo Nanao, Tetsuya Noda, Minoru Ohira and Yutaka Yoshinaga.

FRAENKEL GALLERY
49 Geary St. at Grant, 4th floor / 981-2661

Fraenkel represents 19th and 20th century photographers, including Irving Penn, Robert Mapplethorpe, Eadweard Muybridge, Diane Arbus, Helen Levitt and Edward Weston.

GALLERY PAULE ANGLIM
14 Geary St. at Kearny / 433-2710

Gallery Paule Anglim features contemporary painting and sculpture by Deborah Butterfield, Christopher Brown, Terry Allen, Dawn Fryling and John Beech, among others.

HARCOURTS GALLERY
460 Bush St. at Grant / 421-3428

Harcourts Gallery exhibits works by 19th and 20th century artists, including Pablo Picasso, Joan Miro, Henri Matisse, Renoir, Jasper Johns and Robert Motherwell.

JOHN BERGGRUEN GALLERY
228 Grant Ave. at Post / 781-4629

John Berggruen specializes in 20th century paintings, drawings, sculpture and prints, with exhibitions by such modern masters as Henri Matisse, Henry Moore and Georgia O'Keefe.

THE JOHN PENCE GALLERY
750 Post St. at Jones / 441-1138

The John Pence Gallery specializes in contemporary American realism and large-scale sculpture by artists such as Will Wilson, Michael Lynch, Randall Lake and Donald Davis.

INTERIORS

K KIMPTON GALLERY
228 Grant Ave. at Post, 5th floor / 956-6661

Established and emerging American artists are represented here with paintings, sculptures and prints.

LA PARISIENNE
460 Post St. at Powell / 788-2255

When you enter this boutique, you are transported to Paris in the 1890s — even the doors, counters and painted glass ceiling are original antiques. What many don't know is that in addition to its unique jewelry collection, La Parisienne showcases a fascinating array of turn-of-the-century French posters by such artists as Cheret, Pal, Steinlen, Cappiello and many others. You will also find a wide variety of antique papers, including fans, perfume and wine labels, postcards and small bistro signs. It's heaven on earth for the Francophile!
Closed Sunday

MAXINE'S
3232 Sacramento St. at Presidio / 776-7160

If you appreciate the beauty and craftsmanship of artisans' jewelry, Maxine's is a gallery you shouldn't miss. Located in the renovated carriage room of an 1896 Victorian, the gallery itself is a jewel-toned setting in dark reds and greens. Dramatic interior lighting sets off the works of world-renowned artisans. Long-term exhibits have included the porcelain face pins of Roberta Hanson, the metals of Susan Silver Brown, beadwork by Lucia Antonelli and the fiber arts of Tina Johnson DePuy and Theodora Elston. You'll also discover new artists in limited monthly exhibits.
Closed Sunday

MAXWELL GALLERIES LTD.
551 Sutter St. at Powell / 421-5193

The emphasis here is on early American landscape, American impressionist and French post-impressionist paintings, including a selection of early California paintings.

MICHAEL DUNEV GALLERY
77 Geary St. at Grant / 398-7300

Michael Dunev specializes in paintings, drawings, sculpture and prints by contemporary American and European masters.

MODERNISM
685 Market St. at Kearny / 541-0461

Modernism features masters of modern art of the Russian avant-garde, futurism, German expressionism, and American modern art movements.

MONTGOMERY GALLERY
250 Sutter St. at Kearny, 2nd floor / 788-8300

The Montgomery Gallery showcases California landscapes, French and American impressionists, British and American watercolors and Western scenes.

PASQUALE IANNETTI ART GALLERIES
522 Sutter St. at Powell / 433-2771

Original prints from the 16th century to the present range from Rembrandt etchings and Durer woodcuts to Picasso ceramics and Chagall lithographs.

ROBERT KOCH GALLERY
49 Geary St. at Kearny, 5th floor / 421-0122

Robert Koch Gallery carries an extensive collection of 19th and 20th century photography.

SANTA FE/ART OF THE AMERICAS
3571 Sacramento St. at Locust / 346-0180

In addition to an ever-growing collection of Latin American art, Santa Fe specializes in Edward Curtis photogravures and Ed Borein etchings. Santa Fe is the country's largest source for handsome original silver pieces by William Spratling as well as other antique Mexican jewelry. The gallery also features fine collections of early Navajo and Mexican textiles, Pueblo pottery, contemporary and traditional Southwestern jewelry, Indian baskets, antique furniture, Robert Rivera gourds, resource books and a variety of other beautiful gifts in all price ranges.
Closed Sunday; open daily November & December

STEPHEN WIRTZ GALLERY
49 Geary St. at Kearny, 3rd floor / 433-6879

Stephen Wirtz Gallery exhibits and represents contemporary painting, sculpture and photography with an emphasis on Bay Area artists. Noted among those represented are Richard Avedon, Suzanne Caporael, Michael Kenna, Deborah Oropallo, Arnaldo Pomodoro and Raymond Saunders.
Closed Sunday & Monday

VISION GALLERY
1155 Mission St. at 7th / 621-2107

Vision Gallery has been presenting vintage and contemporary fine art photographs in San Francisco for more than 15 years. With four main galleries and a special Vintage Room, Vision is one of the largest photography galleries in the country. Artists represented include Ansel Adams, Ruth Bernhard, Harry Callahan, Keith Carter, Robert Doisneau, Neil Folberg, Oliver Gagliani, Emmet Gowin, Flor Garduño, William Garnett, Mario Cravo Neto, Jeanloup Sieff, Brett Weston and Don Worth, among many others.
Closed Sunday

WILLIAM SAWYER GALLERY
3045 Clay St. at Baker / 921-1600

William Sawyer represents Northern California artists such as Brian Isobe, David Izu, Rik Ritchey and Barbara Spring.

THERE'S
ONLY
ONE GUIDE
YOU
REALLY
NEED...

Your Passport

to Northern

California

SAN FRANCISCANS ARE THE MOST EUROPEAN OF AMERICANS IN THEIR APPROACH to beauty and fashion. They are stylish, but not trendy — in fact, they are more on the conservative side. With the largest cross-section of cultures in the world, San Francisco is a city that celebrates beauty of all kinds.

In San Francisco, women change their hairstyles and makeup from A.M. to P.M. The openings of the ballet, symphony and opera, the many charity events, dinners at favorite restaurants or someone's home, all are reasons to dress up. Children are just as eager to put on that party dress or suit, whether they're attending *The Nutcracker* or having tea at the Ritz-Carlton.

Introduced by Lee Bledsoe

Lee Bledsoe owns Mister Lee
Beauty, Hair & Health Spa,
one of San Francisco's most elegant
and respected full-service salons.

It's easy to look good here. The beautiful bay and hills bring the softest summer fog to shield both skin and hair from dryness. Too bad if you have curly hair and want to keep it straight — or straight hair and want to keep it curly!

To keep in shape, San Franciscans have a choice of beautiful places to walk or run, with paths through Golden Gate Park, the Marina Green and along the bay, and views you never tire of. Not only do many San Francisco hotels have workout studios, but there are also health clubs throughout the city.

Health & Beauty

Pampering and relaxation are San Francisco rituals. You'll find every kind of service for hair, skin, nails and body. At Mister Lee, we introduced the city's first hydrotherapy treatments using ocean seaweed, aromatherapy oils, vitamins and minerals. Today, our salon is proud to be serving a fourth generation of clients, who maintain the San Francisco tradition of style and fitness. So feel free to dress up and be a San Franciscan!

Thank you: Hotel Nikko; Andy Marshall, EPIC Models

GOLFING BREAKTHROUGH INCREASES LONG DRIVES

BioVision is the world's most advanced Swing Analysis System using computer generated data and graphics to analyze the golf swing as never before possible. BioVision creates a three dimensional picture of your actual golf swing accurate to within one-hundredth of an inch. Golfers are driving from all over to utilize our program which provides you with a half hour VHS tape of your swing with professional analysis from one of our PGA staff and drills to correct the problems. Whether you are a novice, touring pro, or anywhere in between . . . BioVision can show you a truly new exciting and valid way to improve your game.

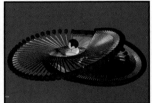

For more information or an appointment, call Optimum Human Performance Center at 1-800-866-3463 or 415-233-7900. Bring this ad with you for a $50 discount.

The new driving force in golf instruction.

FULL SERVICE SALONS

BEAUTY BODY WELLNESS
2325 Third St., Suites 321 & 322 / 626-4685

Although it's off the beaten path, Beauty Body Wellness day spa deserves exploration. Individually prescribed treatments are the specialty. Personalized corrective facials, aromatherapy, seaweed body treatments, nutrition counseling, manicures, pedicures, massages, custom-blended hair and skincare products, make-up, expert haircare — who could ask for anything more? Well, you could ask for all-natural ingredients, a juice bar and a splendid view, but the salon has those too.
Closed Sunday & Monday

BIBBO AT UNION SQUARE
260 Stockton St., 3rd floor / 421-BIBO

A clean, open and airy place to indulge in European facials, manicures, pedicures, waxing and any hair treatment under the sun.

DAVID OLIVER HAIR STUDIO
3356 Sacramento St. at Presidio / 563-2044

Englishman Oliver Creasey has more than two decades of experience in cultivating European hair care for fashion-conscious women and men. His salon caters to a diverse clientele and is staffed with superior stylists and color/perm technicians. Skin care, nail care, aromatherapy and hair care products are also available.
Closed Sunday

DIPIETRO TODD SALON
177 Post St. at Grant, 2nd floor / 397-0177

A spectacular open loft with distressed wood floors, theatrical lighting and a beverage bar houses the largest privately owned salon in Northern California.

I. MAGNIN BEAUTY SALON
135 Stockton St. at Geary / 781-7760

A large staff provides total head-to-toe pampering, including hair and nail services, makeup analysis and application, facials and body waxing.

LEW GALLO
140 Geary St. at Stockton, Suite 700 / 296-7424

The largest non-rental salon in the city, Lew Gallo sets a young, exciting and energetic tone. Pampering takes place against a spare, industrial backdrop of exposed cement floors and green stone counters, and includes nail care, facials, makeup and full hair care services. A vast selection of beauty and skincare products is also available for at-home maintenance. Private facilities available.
Closed Sunday & Monday

MACY'S BEAUTYWORKS
Union Square, 4th floor / 954-6363

Beautyworks caters to all ages with every conceivable service for hair, nails, face and body.

MISTER LEE
834 Jones St. at Bush / 474-6002

Known to discerning San Franciscans for four generations, Mister Lee's has built its reputation on expert hair cutting, styling and color. The salon has extended its third floor to become the most complete day spa in the country, with top technology and equipment from around the world, including hydro-jet tub, high-pressure hose shower for cellulite treatment, body sculpting, toning and stress reduction, sea algae and compression wraps, and aromatherapy facials. Full and half-day packages are available.
Closed Sunday

ST. MORITZ
Hyatt Union Square / 421-7022
San Francisco Hilton / 771-1400

Catering to busy professionals, St. Moritz has expert hair services and provides the antidote for stress, from steam or sauna to luxurious therapeutic massages.

SAKS FIFTH AVENUE BEAUTY SALON
384 Post St. at Powell / 986-0576

The spacious, comfortable salon at Saks specializes in pampering both men and women with haircuts, perms, color, manicures, pedicures, waxing and deep cleansing facials with Adrien Arpel products.
Closed Sunday

77 MAIDEN LANE SALON
77 Maiden Lane, 4th floor / 391-7777

77 Maiden Lane Salon's philosophy of beauty for hair, face and body reflects the salon itself, with its bleached oak floors, pink and faux-marble walls, and simply draped windows — a look that is romantic yet modern. More than 20 stylists offer complete hair services, including permanent hair weaving to thicken or length-

HEALTH & BEAUTY

en hair. Manicures and pedicures are offered, and there are private rooms for facials, peelings, eyebrow and eyelash tinting, body waxing and massage. The salon has a complete makeup department for lessons and applications. 77 Maiden Lane also specializes in weddings. *Closed Sunday*

HAIR SALONS

FOCUS HAIR STUDIO
3263 Sacramento St. at Presidio / 931-5205

Whether your personal image is classic or trendy, you can expect complete attention to detail at Focus. The salon's three accomplished designers will give you the proper cut, color or perm to expand and enhance your total look. *Closed Sunday & Monday*

HAIR BY HENRIK & CO.
251 Post St. at Stockton, Suite 306 / 392-1166

Hair by Henrik & Co. features cuts from classic to avant-garde, creating hairstyles that work for the individual man or woman and provide the look of the '90s. Ongoing training here and abroad for the salon's highly accomplished stylists ensures application of contemporary technique and design. Other services include manicures, pedicures and complete makeovers. *Closed Sunday*

HUBERT BRAUN
420 Sutter St. at Powell / 421-1507

Hubert Braun has been providing expert hair services in San Francisco for more than 20 years.

IDIO HAIR STUDIO
3027B Fillmore St. near Union / 931-4400

Surrounded by a garden courtyard, Idio's clients enjoy a relaxing time just a few steps from the hustle and bustle of Union Street. The salon offers up-to-the-minute haircuts, permanents, highlights and styling techniques to suit each client's personal style. Late evening appointments available. *Closed Sunday*

JOHN VELASQUEZ HAIRSTYLING
440 Jackson St. at Sansome / 391-5512

Furnished with Country French antiques, John Velasquez's salon fits right into its historic Jackson Square location.

NICHOLAS STUDIO
Hotel Nikko San Francisco
222 Mason St. at O'Farrell / 982-6565

Nicholas Studio caters to the professional business person. The salon's philosophy is to create a style that suits each client's personality and hair texture. Haircuts are adapted to the individual's facial features and hair

growth pattern, and they are shaped to be trouble-free and easy to duplicate. Nicholas Studio also offers coloring and permanent treatments.
Closed Sunday & Monday

ROY SALON
3384 Sacramento St. at Walnut / 563-9999

Here proprietor Roy Rawlings mixes his progressive Chelsea styling background with classic techniques to produce versatile, modern cuts.

ST. TROPEZ
1980 Union St. at Buchanan, 2nd floor / 563-3514

The new European management of St. Tropez offers you a personalized consultation on the latest techniques for haircuts and styling, as well as highlights, colors and perms. The salon uses two new and natural lines of French products for hair and skin care. St. Tropez pampers each client in a friendly, relaxing Parisian ambiance.
Closed Sunday & by appointment Monday

SIMON, A HAIR SALON
5 Claude Lane at Sutter / 391-4666

Formerly of John London and Atelier 249 in London, Simon Poon is a 20-year veteran in the hair design business. Featuring low-maintenance, simple yet elegant styling for women and men who always want to look distinctive, his salon offers one-stop hair, skin and makeup services.
Closed Sunday & Monday

VIDAL SASSOON
130 Post St. at Grant / 397-5105

Vidal Sassoon salons have been satisfying a diverse clientele since 1955. The newest fashion cuts take into account the texture and fullness of hair and include the geometric shapes that made Sassoon famous.

YOSH FOR HAIR
173 Maiden Lane at Stockton / 989-7704

Since 1971, Yosh for Hair has offered well-rounded hair care and design programs to a devoted clientele.

SKIN CARE & MAKEUP

COREEN CORDOVA COSMETIC SALON
177 Post St. at Grant, 2nd floor / 434-0957

Now in the classy di Pietro Todd Salon, Coreen Cordova analyzes individual makeup needs and charts specific steps for makeup application.

ESTEE LAUDER SPA
I. Magnin Mezzanine, 135 Stockton St. / 403-2147

Synonymous with American glamour and beauty since the 1930s, Estee Lauder has extended its concept to spas

that emphasize full-length skincare with immediate results. The opulent downtown spa, one of ten in the nation, cradles customers with tenderness. A nurturing decor and personalized service enhance the advanced rituals in store, including facials for every skin type, expert makeup applications, waxing and deep-cleansing back therapy for summer baring. Of course, Estee Lauder's full line of cosmetics and treatments can be purchased here as well.
Open daily

THE FACE PLACE/BENEFIT
339 Kearny St. at Bush / 781-8153
2219 Chestnut St. at Pierce / 567-1173
2117 Fillmore St. at California / 567-0242

Twin co-owners Jane Blackford and Jean Danielson manufacture their own water-based, fragrance-free cosmetic and treatment line.

FACES ETCETERA
210 Post St. at Grant, Suite 709 / 788-8817

Shirley Carper's private salon is a world away from urban stress. Individual attention is emphasized in the relaxed, thoroughly professional atmosphere. With its convenient Union Square location, Faces Etcetera has been offering clients personalized attention for more than ten years, providing the absolute best in facials and deep pore cleansing. And that's just the beginning. The staff is thoroughly trained to pamper the rest of you too, from nail care to massage, to help you look and feel your best. Evening appointments also available.
Closed Sunday & Monday

GEORGINA ACOSTA INC.
940 Bush St. at Jones / 885-1551

Georgina Acosta commands a loyal following and has earned a reputation as a first-class facial salon.

LANCOME INSTITUT DE BEAUTE
Macy's, Union Square / 296-4242

Tucked away in Macy's, Lancome Institut de Beaute is an oasis of calm and pampering.

MARY THE SKIN CARE SALON
153 Maiden Lane at Grant / 788-8431

The thorough approach at Mary Thé stresses education with the most scientific, up-to-date treatment. Mary Thé is recognized as one of San Francisco's leading skincare experts. The salon's basic skincare is a 1½-hour session to manually clean pores. The treatment also includes a mild peeling and a soothing mask. Additional services offered are waxing, manicure, pedicure, massage, reflexology, makeup and permanent makeup applications. Mary Thé offers gift certificates and free consultations.
Closed Sunday

77 MAIDEN LANE SALON
77 Maiden Lane, 4th floor / 391-7777

77 Maiden Lane Salon's philosophy of beauty for hair, face and body reflects the salon itself, with its bleached oak floors, pink and faux-marble walls, and simply draped windows — a look that is romantic yet modern. More than 20 stylists offer complete hair services, including permanent hair weaving to thicken or lengthen hair. Manicures and pedicures are offered, and there are private rooms for facials, peelings, eyebrow and eyelash tinting, body waxing and massage. The salon also features a complete makeup department, with lessons, applications and a full line of environmentally conscientious makeup for today's lifestyles. 77 Maiden Lane specializes in weddings.
Closed Sunday

MASSAGE

FOR YOUR BACK ONLY
2906 Lyon St. at Greenwich / 563-1274

Owner Gisele White caters to stressed-out professionals and those in search of simple relaxation, using both light and deep tissue massage to relieve pain from injuries or soothe tired muscles. Certified massage therapists specialize in Swedish massage, Shiatsu, reflexology, pre- and post-natal massage, cellulite massage, lymphatic drainage and body wraps. The massages are available, by appointment only, from 8AM to 8PM.
Closed Sunday

KABUKI HOT SPRING
1750 Geary Blvd. at Fillmore / 922-6000

A traditional Japanese spa and Shiatsu massage center, Kabuki Hot Spring has been helping people relax since 1971. Choose between five plans, ranging from the Sakura Plan, with unlimited use of the communal hot and cold baths, to the Shogun Plan, including private Japanese-style bath, steam cabinet or sauna and a 55-minute massage.
Open daily

HEALTH CLUBS

BAY CLUB/BANK OF AMERICA CENTER
555 California St. at Montgomery / 362-7800

The newest addition to the Bay Club family, Bay Club/ Bank of America Center is conveniently located in the heart of the Financial District. Busy executives can work off stress just minutes away from their offices at this premier fitness facility, with its superb service and broad range of exercise classes and equipment. Or they can simply relax in the luxurious sauna, steam room or whirlpool spa before catching some tanning salon rays.

BAY CLUB/MARATHON PLAZA
303 2nd St. at Folsom / 543-9100

Surrounded by plentiful windows and light, members of this Financial District fitness center enjoy challenging aerobics and conditioning workouts designed for a busy clientele. Unique to San Francisco clubs, the "exerflex" floor reflects a low-impact training awareness and is built to give, reducing chance of injury. Cybex equipment and a broad range of classes make this San Francisco Bay Club extension a condensed exercise facility for people who want to stay fit with convenience. Shuttle service available.

CATHEDRAL HILL PLAZA ATHLETIC CLUB
1333 Gough St. at Geary / 346-4929

The Plaza Club offers full-circuit training equipment, free weights, computerized bicycles, rowing machines, two lighted tennis courts and a host of pampering amenities. Exercise classes are held in both the aerobic studio and the 20-yard indoor pool. Monthly limited and unlimited memberships available.

CITY GYM OF SAN FRANCISCO
50 1st St. at Market, 2nd floor / 882-4411

City Gym's result-oriented workouts are designed to get you in the best shape possible.

GOLD'S GYM
501 2nd St. at Bryant / 777-GOLD

Gold's Gym in San Francisco enhances its international reputation as a bodybuilding facility with aerobics, saunas and suntanning beds in addition to their famous "world-class" weight training. Memberships of virtually any duration are available, as are corporate and "Preferred Gold" memberships.

GOLDEN GATEWAY TENNIS AND SWIM CLUB
370 Drumm St., Golden Gateway Center / 433-2936

Golden Gateway is two clubs in one: a tennis club with nine courts, and a health club with Lifecycles, StairMasters, free weights, treadmills, whirlpool, sauna, steam and a heated 55-foot outdoor lap pool.

NIKKO FITNESS CENTER
Hotel Nikko San Francisco
222 Mason St. at O'Farrell / 394-1153

This health club has a full fitness room with free weights, Lifecycles, treadmill, rowing machines and Maxicam equipment. A personal trainer and a 16-meter glass-enclosed swimming pool are also available, along with jacuzzi, tanning facilities, massage and sauna. Open to the public, Nikko Fitness Center offers daily, monthly and annual rates.

HEALTH & BEAUTY

NOB HILL CLUB
950 California St. at Powell / 397-2770

Located in the Fairmont Hotel, the Nob Hill Club is a health and fitness club available for daily use to guests of the Fairmont and guests of other hotels. The facilities include a full line of Nautilus, free weights and instruction, aerobics, Lifecycles, exercycles, treadmills, rowing machines, steam, sauna and jacuzzi.

PACIFIC HEIGHTS HEALTH CLUB
2358 Pine St. at Fillmore / 563-6694

The Pacific Heights Club offers Nautilus, free weights, massage, suntanning, weight training instruction, cardiovascular conditioning, towel service and full spa (dry sauna, steam room and jacuzzi). Facilities are open to both men and women. Monthly, annual and daily rates.

PINNACLE FITNESS
135 Post St. at Kearny / 781-7343

Pinnacle Fitness is the perfect downtown getaway, offering a wide range of health and beauty options. Special services include massage, suntanning and hair care at the club's salon. Join for a month, a year or take advantage of the club's special daily rates, and you can use in-shape free weights, Icarian and Iso Flex circuit-training machines, StairMasters, Climbmax Stair Climbers, Lifecycles, Windracers, recumbent bikes, Versaclimber, Startrac treadmills, Gravatron, Concept 2 Rowers, rooftop jogging track, sundeck and a four-lane lap pool. Certified personal trainers can help you with your workouts, and you can choose from 10 daily aerobic classes. There are separate facilities for men and women, in addition to co-ed.

PLAZA ATHLETIC CLUB AT MUSEUM PARC
350 Third St. at Folsom / 543-8466

The Plaza Athletic Club is everything a downtown health facility should be: it opens early every day, is conveniently located for city residents and commuters, and offers state-of-the-art equipment and the latest in conditioning, weight training and aerobics classes. Clean locker, sauna and steam rooms, heated outdoor lap pool, cardiovascular center, personal trainers and massage services are also available.

SAN FRANCISCO ATHLETIC CLUB
1755 O'Farrell St. at Fillmore / 776-2260

The San Francisco Athletic Club offers a wide variety of exercise options. The club has a five-lane, 25-yard pool and a water aerobics class. Members can enjoy the club's sport courts, then relax with a massage, spa or steam. A complete selection of cardiovascular activities includes StairMaster and treadmill equipment, and you can choose from many types of exercise classes from step, yoga and low-impact to street jam. For strength enhancement, the San Francisco Athletic Club provides

a variety of machines and free weights. Free garage parking. Daily, monthly and annual memberships.

SAN FRANCISCO BAY CLUB
150 Greenwich St. at Sansome / 433-2200

The Bay Club has every sport and activity imaginable: two tennis courts, three racquetball courts, nine squash courts, a basketball court, two five-lane 22-yard pools, Nautilus and Cybex machines, Lifecycles, StairMasters, treadmills, rowing machines and newly expanded free-weight and locker rooms. Take one of fifteen daily aerobic classes, then have a massage, get a suntan and revive yourself with a healthy snack in their cafe. Beauty services also available. Before starting an exercise program, stop at the club's sports medicine facility. Memberships only.

SAN FRANCISCO TENNIS CLUB
645 5th St. at Brannan / 777-9000

Tennis, sports and fitness are the main attractions of this private membership club with 28 indoor and outdoor tennis courts.

SHEEHAN POOL & FITNESS CENTER
620 Sutter St. at Mason / 775-6500

Located in the Sheehan Hotel, near Union Square, the fitness center has an indoor heated lap pool with a full program of swimming lessons, water aerobics and master swim sessions. The workout room includes Nautilus and Universal weight machines, treadmill, rowing machine, Stairclimber and exercise bicycles. The fitness center has no membership dues. A day fee of $4 covers towel and locker services; discount passes and monthly lockers are available for a longer use of the facility.

TELEGRAPH HILL CLUB
1850 Kearny St. at Chestnut / 543-7992

A very modern interior, six aerobic classes a day, racquetball courts, a basketball court, sauna and whirlpool for men and women, and an aerobic exercise center that includes Airdynes, StairMasters, Lifecycles, treadmills, exercycles and rowing machines — these are only the beginning. There's a restaurant too, not to mention a manicurist and massage therapist. One-time membership with monthly dues.

24-HOUR NAUTILUS
1335 Sutter St. at Van Ness / 776-2200

All kinds of fitness machines and an aerobics studio are the attractions here.

AEROBIC CLUBS

FITNESS BREAK
30 Hotaling Pl. at Jackson / 788-1681

High-and low-impact and combination aerobics, step

classes and circuit training, body conditioning and weight training in the Financial District.

IN SHAPE
2328 Fillmore St. at Washington / 346-5660
3214 Fillmore St. at Greenwich / 922-3700

Two locations, same great classes: aerobics, low-impact, high/low impact, body conditioning with weights, and Move, a high-energy, low-impact workout.

JAZZERCISE
Various locations / 561-9300

High-energy choreographed exercise classes for all levels, by the folks who began the aerobics dance craze.

RHYTHM & MOTION
Various locations / 621-0643

Vigorous choreographed workouts that avoid jarring and pounding, all taught by professional dancers.

SANTE WEST
3727 Buchanan St. at Bay / 563-6222

Step classes, aerobics, body sculpting, and a super conditioner, the Cardio program.

25TH STREET WORKOUT
1500 Castro St. at 25th / 647-1224

A friendly studio for high- and low-impact aerobics, body sculpting, step and stretch classes.

TANNING SALONS

BROWNIE'S EUROPEAN TANNING
1735 Union St. at Gough / 775-3815

San Francisco's leading salon for 14 years, Brownie's has five tanning beds that feature Silver Solarium and the Wolff System, five-track stereo, student and mid-day discounts and the patented Thermo Trim Inch Loss System. The salon is located in the heart of Pacific Heights and the Marina. Be sure to request a personalized "browning" schedule. Brownie's is open daily and offers specials for visitors from out of town.

THE CABANA CLUB
3151 Fillmore St. at Greenwich / 922-2262

The Cabana Club is the largest tanning salon in the city. Open 18 hours a day.

COCOTAN
837 Irving St. at 9th / 566-1018

Cocotan offers six Vitasun beds and an introductory discount for new clients.

GREAT TAN
3248 Sacramento St. at Presidio / 922-2214

For an honest, no-frills tan at a reasonable price, try Great Tan's Silver Solarium and Jetson High Speed systems.

GOLD'S GYM®

Results for every $BODY$

501 Second Street at Bryant
San Francisco, CA 94107
(415) 777·GOLD

HEALTH & BEAUTY

SOMEWHERE BACK IN THE 1970S, THE MEDIA HUNG AN IMAGE ON MARIN COUNTY, an image of wealth and the fast life, of hot tubs, peacock feathers and high-end mortgages. Times have changed, yet the media holds on to its stereotypes, missing the real beauty and fascination of this place.

Marin's majesty is in its landscape — a grand interplay of mountains and redwood valleys, ocean vistas and the curving shores of San Francisco Bay. Just to reach Marin, you must cross the magnificent Golden Gate Bridge or ferry across from San Francisco.

Undulating northward from the Golden Gate through a series of low hills is Highway 101. It is known as "the corridor" in county planning circles, and most of Marin's development surrounds it. Driving west, you will find bucolic valleys and ocean views, small towns and rolling coastal roadways. To the east, wilderness and park lands border the bay.

It is Marin's unique blend of urban corridor and rural tranquility that is so attractive to both visitors and residents. Marin is not a faceless suburbia. Each town has its own identity, separated from its neighbors by hills and history.

Take the ferryboat to Sausalito, Larkspur or Tiburon, bicycle through Mill Valley or Ross, hike the trails of Mt. Tamalpais, or simply drink in the views. They are what makes Marin so special.

Introduced by Phil Frank

Phil Frank is the creator of the comic strip "Farley," which appears daily in the San Francisco Chronicle, *and of the "Chateau Dafitte" comic, which appears in the* Wine Spectator.

Although he has lived in Sausalito with his wife Susan for 21 years, he is still considered a newcomer by old-time residents. His studio is a pilot house on an 1880s ferryboat in Sausalito's houseboat community. Mr. Frank is currently chairman of the Sausalito Historical Society.

Thank you: Kristin La Fontaine, D.C., City Models

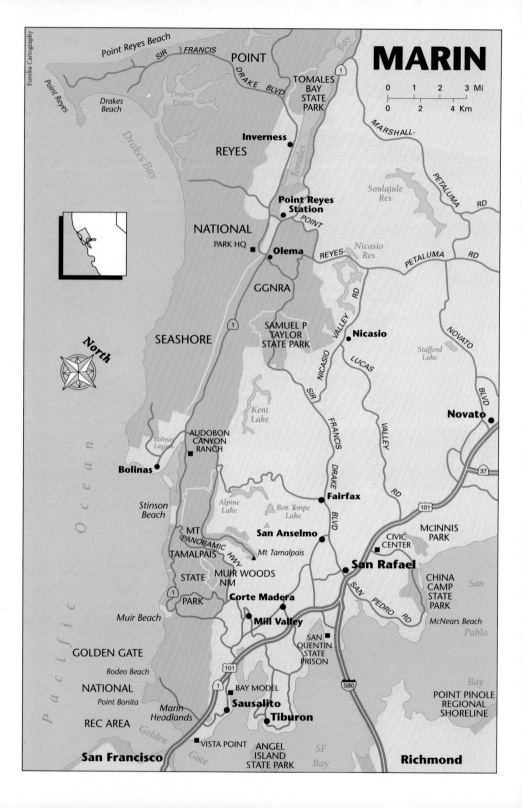

MARIN

Point Reyes Beach

SIR FRANCIS DRAKE BLVD

POINT

TOMALES
BAY
STATE
PARK

Point Reyes

*Drakes
Beach*

*Drakes
Estero*

MARSHALL-

Inverness

REYES

Drakes Bay

*Soulajule
Res*

PETALUMA RD

**Point Reyes
Station**

POINT

*Nicasio
Res*

NATIONAL

PARK HQ

Olema

REYES

PETALUMA RD

GGNRA

**SAMUEL P
TAYLOR
STATE PARK**

NICASIO

VALLEY RD

Nicasio

NOVATO

*Stafford
Lake*

SEASHORE

LUCAS

North

*Kent
Lake*

SIR

VALLEY RD

BLVD

Novato

*Bolinas
Lagoon*

**AUDOBON
CANYON
RANCH**

FRANCIS

37

Bolinas

*Alpine
Lake*

*Bon Tempe
Lake*

Fairfax

DRAKE

RD

101

*Stinson
Beach*

San Anselmo

BLVD

**McINNIS
PARK**

MT

PANORAMIC HWY

▲ *Mt Tamalpais*

CIVIC
CENTER

TAMALPAIS

**MUIR WOODS
NM**

San Rafael

**CHINA
CAMP
STATE
PARK**

STATE

1

Corte Madera

SAN

McNears Beach

*San
Pablo*

PARK

Mill Valley

PEDRO

Muir Beach

SAN
QUENTIN
STATE
PRISON

RD

Bay

GOLDEN GATE

101

Rodeo Beach

580

**POINT PINOLE
REGIONAL
SHORELINE**

NATIONAL

1

BAY MODEL

Point Bonita

Sausalito

REC AREA

*Marin
Headlands*

Tiburon

■ VISTA POINT

**ANGEL
ISLAND
STATE PARK**

*SF
Bay*

Golden

San Francisco

Gate

Richmond

Pacific Ocean

Tomales Bay

0	1	2	3 Mi
0	2	4 Km	

MARIN INFORMATION

AAA EMERGENCY ROAD SERVICE
Northern Marin 461-0415
Southern Marin 924-1680

BICYCLE RENTALS
Ken's Bike Shop, Tiburon...........................435-1683
Point Reyes Procyclery................................663-1046

BOAT RENTALS
Cass' Marina, Sausalito 332-6789
Powerboat Rental with Capt. Case, Sausalito
....331-0444

BUS SERVICE
Golden Gate Bus Transit 332-6600

FERRY SERVICE
Golden Gate Ferry Service 332-6600
Red & White Fleet 546-2896

GOLF COURSES
Indian Valley Golf Course, Novato 897-1118
Mill Valley Municipal Course.....................388-9982
Peacock Gap, San Rafael 453-4122

HORSEBACK RIDING
Five Brooks Stables, Olema........................663-1570
Miwok Livery, Mill Valley...........................383-8048

SHOPPING CENTERS
• Corte Madera Town Center
• Larkspur Landing, Larkspur
• Northgate Mall, San Rafael
• Strawberry Village, Mill Valley
• Village at Corte Madera

TAXIS
Belaire Taxi..383-8484
Sausalito Taxi 383-0640

WINDSURFING
Sausalito Sailboards 331-9463
Windsports, San Rafael..............................459-1171

MARIN DIRECTORY

POINTS OF INTEREST

THE BAY AREA DISCOVERY MUSEUM
557 E. Fort Baker at Murray Circle, Sausalito / 332-7674

The Bay Area Discovery Museum is a hands-on museum located in a spectacular setting at East Fort Baker, on the north side of the Golden Gate Bridge. Its historic buildings house the permanent "San Francisco Bay" and "Building the City" exhibitions and art studio. Kids will love the fishing boat that rocks, the mock underwater tunnel and the special art and science classes. Don't miss the new Tot Spot for kids under three. In the summer, the museum sponsors nature hikes, face painting and drop-in art and theatre workshops. The Birthday Room may be reserved for parties. The rental includes free admission, party favors, table decorations and a special gift for the birthday child. This summer the museum will add a children's outdoor sculpture garden and two new buildings, with such interesting new exhibits as "The World of Jim Henson: Muppets, Monsters and Magic."
Open 10AM to 5PM Tuesday through Sunday in summer; 10AM to 5PM Wednesday through Sunday in winter

BAY MODEL
2100 Bridgeway at Spring, Sausalito / 332-3871

This hydraulic model of San Francisco Bay and the Sacramento River Delta takes up a three-acre building on the northern outskirts of Sausalito. Built by the U.S. Army Corps of Engineers in 1956, the model predicts the impact of new construction projects on San Francisco Bay. Using the model, a year's worth of bay activity can be condensed into three days — a boon in times of disaster such as an oil spill. Guided and self-guided tours, as well as free audio tours in four different languages, are available. No admission charge.
Open 9AM to 4PM Tuesday through Saturday in winter; 9AM to 4PM Tuesday through Friday and 10AM to 6PM Saturday & Sunday in summer and on holidays

MARIN HEADLANDS
From Hwy. 101 take the Alexander Ave. Exit / 331-1540

Overlooking the entrance to San Francisco Bay, these steep, windswept hillsides offer magnificent views of the Golden Gate Bridge and the city skyline as well as great panoramas of the Pacific Ocean. Stop at the National Park Service Visitors Center at the intersection of Bunker and Field roads (five miles west of the Golden Gate Bridge) for maps and information. Visit the Marine Mammal Rehabilitation Center, which treats wounded seals and sea lions washed up on surrounding shores. Call ahead if you want to visit Point Bonita Lighthouse.
Primitive camping & hostel accommodations nearby

MOUNT TAMALPAIS STATE PARK
Marin County / 388-2070

The undulating mountain-line profile, as seen from the

MARIN

bay side, resembles a Sleeping Maiden, known affectionately as "Mt. Tam." This 6,400-acre park is a favorite hiking and picnicking treasure for visitors and Bay Area residents. Trails lead through grasslands, chaparral, oak savannah, redwood forests, windswept ridges and deep canyon creeks. Dogs are not allowed on trails. On a clear day the summit of Mt. Tam (2,571 feet) affords a view of the entire Bay Area. Hold on to your hats up there!
Open sunrise to sunset in winter; 7AM to 10PM in summer

MUIR WOODS NATIONAL MONUMENT
From Hwy. 101, take the Hwy. One-Stinson Beach Exit
388-2595
Some of these incredible trees grow to heights of over 250 feet. This world-famous stand of virgin coastal redwood was donated in 1908 by William Kent in honor of naturalist John Muir. No picnicking is allowed, but a cafe and visitor's center can be found near the parking lot. About 40 minutes by car from the city. Pets are not permitted in the park.
Open 8AM to sunset daily

POINT REYES NATIONAL SEASHORE
Point Reyes / 663-1092
An hour from the city (take Sir Francis Drake Boulevard in San Rafael to Highway One), the spectacular Point Reyes peninsula offers windswept beaches and some of the most varied plant and animal life in Northern California. Hiking trails — from an easy flat path down to the beach through wildflower meadows and tall trees to steep chaparral trails ending in remote campgrounds — crisscross the land. Limantour Beach, one of Marin's loveliest beaches, is nearly always empty, a great place to be alone with the birds and sea lions. Those who prefer driving can head for Point Reyes Lighthouse, popular as a lookout for whales during the winter months. Tomales Bay, the inlet separating Point Reyes from the mainland, has beaches as well as a thriving oyster industry.

SAUSALITO CHAMBER OF COMMERCE
333 Caledonia St. at Litho, Sausalito / 332-0505
Spanish explorer Juan Manuel de Ayala discovered Sausalito, then home to the Miwok Indians, in 1775 and is credited for naming it Saucelito, or little willow. Visitors today stop at the Sausalito Chamber of Commerce before embarking on their own exploration of this historical area. The Chamber supplies detailed information about points of interest, ferryboat schedules, lodging, boutiques, yacht clubs, restaurants, galleries, events and much more. The Chamber also sponsors one of the nation's premier art events, the annual Sausalito Art Festival, which draws more than 60,000 tourists to Sausalito over the Labor Day weekend.
Open 9AM to 5PM Monday through Friday

STINSON BEACH
From Hwy. 101, take the Hwy. One-Stinson Beach Exit
868-0942
For all you beach lovers looking for golden stretches of sand with pounding white surf against an azure sky, head for Stinson Beach downhill from Mt. Tam. Most people come to sunbathe, though in the southern portion lying within the Golden Gate National Recreation Area, lifeguards keep an eye on those who brave chilly waters. The rocky headland is also a popular fishing spot. Picnic facilities are available.
Open 9AM to about an hour after sunset daily

TIBURON
The Tiburon peninsula projects out into the bay, offering fortunate residents a sweeping view of the city and the Golden Gate Bridge. Picturesque, prosperous and private, Tiburon offers visitors a look at Marin County's "good life." A cluster of restaurants and bars hugs the shoreline; a favorite pastime of both locals and visitors is to lunch, brunch or drink on one of the outdoor terraces extending out over the water. Beware of pesky seagulls who often swoop down for a bite of hamburger, whether you've finished it or not! Stylish boutiques and unique gift shops line Main Street and Ark Row, a string of converted houseboats now land-bound and popular for browsing and whiling away a sunny afternoon. Though Tiburon can be reached by car, the nicest way to get there is by taking the ferry from Fisherman's Wharf.

WINDSOR VINEYARDS
72 Main St., Tiburon / 435-3113
Windsor Vineyards has quietly won the most awards of any winery in America for five years in a row. Thirty minutes from San Francisco by car or by Red & White Ferry service, the tasting room is a block from waterfront restaurants and shops. Windsor Vineyards has 35 wines available for complimentary tastings. The Tiburon tasting room has validated parking next door in the Main Street lot. The winery also has a tasting room in Healdsburg. Both offer unique personalized labels for Windsor Vineyards gift sets.
Open Sunday through Thursday 10AM to 6PM, Saturday & Sunday 10AM to 7PM

EXCURSIONS

CASS' MARINA
1702 Bridgeway at Napa, Sausalito / 332-6789
Pier 39, San Francisco / 800-4-SAIL95
Navigating a sailboat on demanding San Francisco Bay requires great skill. Cass' Marina's classes for individuals and groups of all ages instill respect for this exhilarating sport, and their charters and rentals appeal to "old salts" and initiates alike. All boats are equipped

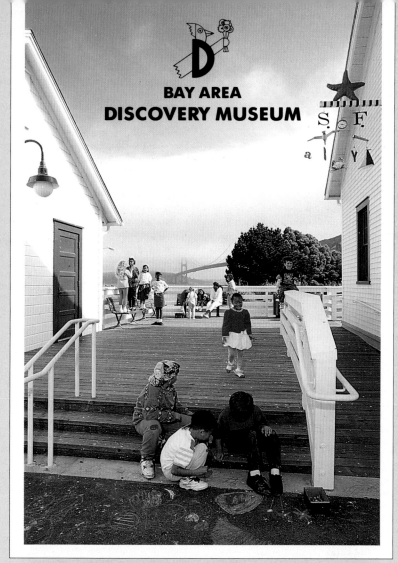

BAY AREA
DISCOVERY MUSEUM

EXPLORE!

EXPERIMENT!

LEARN!

INVENT!

DANCE!

BUILD!

CREATE!

DRAW!

SING!

A CHILDREN'S MUSEUM FOR THE WHOLE FAMILY
East Fort Baker, Sausalito   Phone 415/332-7674

- **THE MEDIA CENTER**
- **THE SCIENCE LAB**
- **LIVE PERFORMANCES**
- **SPECIAL BIRTHDAY PARTIES**
- **"THE HEART OF HOME"**
  (August '93 - January '94) featuring kitchens
  from Thailand, Mexico and Greece!
- **COMING IN JANUARY '94: THE MUPPETS!**

- **ARCHITECTURE AND BAY HALLS**
- **SUMMER CAMPS**
- **OUTDOOR ADVENTURES:** nature
  hikes, tide pooling, whale watching,
  camping trips
- **MAZE OF ILLUSIONS**
- **ART PROJECTS GALORE!**
- **TRANSPORTATION CENTER**

with Coast-Guard required gear, and larger boats are outfitted for overnight cruising. Established in 1961, Cass' also arranges sailing vacations to the Caribbean, South Pacific or Mediterranean.

POWERBOAT RENTAL WITH CAPT. CASE
1702 Bridgeway at Napa, Sausalito / 331-0444

The Bay Area's exclusive powerboat rental source, Capt. Case's features unsinkable Boston Whaler powerboats, available with or without a captain. You can enjoy an excursion from two hours to a full day, with a pickup on San Francisco's waterfront at your request.

GALLERIES

FINE ART COLLECTIONS
686 Bridgeway near Princess, Sausalito / 331-0500

On the waterfront, Fine Art Collections is devoted to world-renowned artists such as Erte and Isaac Maimon. The gallery specializes in assisting clients interested in building private collections.

GALLERY PIAZZA
819 Bridgeway, north of Village Fair, 3rd floor
Sausalito Piazza Building, Sausalito / 331-6711

Gallery Piazza, Arts & Culture serves a dual purpose as a center for intercultural dialogue and creativity and as a display for contemporary fine arts. A progressive gallery, Piazza exhibits works by local, national and international artists. The artists featured include Shioh Kato, Koichi Tanikawa, Heather Wilcoxon, Valentin Popov, Thomas Bayrle and numerous Native American artists. Works by modern masters such as Picasso, Miro and Max Ernst are also available. With its design, atmosphere and spectacular views of the Sausalito Harbor and San Francisco Bay, Gallery Piazza is also an excellent space for conferences, lectures and workshops.
Open 11AM to 6PM Thursday through Sunday; other days by appointment

HANSON GALLERIES
669 Bridgeway at Princess, Sausalito / 332-3078

Hanson Galleries displays the work of nationally and internationally known contemporary artists in changing exhibits. Hanson also has a gallery in San Francisco.

SHOPPING

BARCELINO
819 Bridgeway, north of Village Fair
Sausalito / 331-0773

Recognized for its fine quality European men's apparel and elegant neo-Romanesque store interiors, Barcelino offers the finest collection of international menswear in the Bay Area. The all-European clothing ranges from formal wear to business wear to sportswear, including a broad selection of designs by Belvest, Canali, Lubiam, Ravazzolo and others. Sophisticated, fashion-conscious men appreciate the clothing's natural fibers and classic, Continental styling. Other Barcelino locations include stores at the Fairmont and the Stouffer Stanford Court hotels in San Francisco, 498 Post Street in San Francisco, the Stanford Shopping Center in Palo Alto, the Valley Fair Mall in San Jose and the Sunvalley Mall in Concord.
Open daily & by appointment

DAVID HURLEY GOLDSMITHS
30 Princess St. off Bridgeway, Sausalito / 332-3401

David Hurley, Sausalito's master goldsmith, is renowned for his stonecutting techniques and the originality of his exquisite designs.

GENE HILLER
Sausalito / 332-3636

Gene Hiller has been a leading California resource for exclusive menswear since 1956. An elegant setting and on-premise tailoring add to the shopping enjoyment.

HEATH CERAMICS
400 Gate Five Rd. at Bridgeway, Sausalito / 332-3732

A pottery studio and stoneware factory outlet, Heath Ceramics molds, spins and glazes mud and clay into classic California-style dinnerware and tiles.

LYZ
1020 Magnolia Ave., Larkspur / 461-0777

Chic women from all over the Bay Area have depended on Lily Samii to dress them in the finest American and European couture. Outfits are brought out a few at a time and carefully accessorized by a professional staff.

PEGASUS LEATHER
28/30 Princess St. off Bridgeway, Sausalito
Women's shop 332-5624 / Men's shop 332-1718

Pegasus's broad selection of men's and women's classic leather and suede coats, skirts, dresses, jackets, boots and accessories will enhance any look and lifestyle.

ROMANCE & ROSES
15 E. Blithedale at Throckmorton
Mill Valley / 381-2270

Located in the center of charming Mill Valley, Romance & Roses offers the finest linen and accessories for the bed and bath. Here, romance is never forgotten, and the focus is always on elegance and excellence. You'll find bath towels from England, Scotland and Portugal, handmade quilts from Kentucky and sheets from Italy and the United States. With a touch of lace here and a whiff of scent there, Romance & Roses creates the perfect atmosphere for your shopping pleasure.
Open daily & by appointment

TIMBERLAND
668 Bridgeway at Princess, Sausalito / 332-1096

Here you'll find the Timberland Company's entire line of rugged clothing, from handsewn hiking boots, sandals and bucks to casual skirts, trousers, sweaters and shirts.

SHOPPING CENTERS

THE VILLAGE AT CORTE MADERA
1554 Redwood Hwy. at Paradise Dr. & Hwy. 101
Corte Madera / 924-8557

Located in scenic Southern Marin, The Village at Corte Madera is a truly unique shopping experience. The beautifully designed open-air center is distinguished as much by its lush landscaping and contemporary architecture as by its distinctive collection of stores, including more than 90 shops. **Nordstrom, Macy's, AnnTaylor, Eddie Bauer, Gap, Nature Company, Crate & Barrel** and many other specialty stores provide the best in fashions, home interiors, gifts and specialty items. The selection of restaurants and cafes offers a bounty of international cuisines for a quick bite or for more leisurely dining. At The Village at Corte Madera, shopping is as relaxed and inviting as Marin itself.

Open Monday through Friday 10AM to 9PM, Saturday 10AM to 6PM, Sunday noon to 6PM. Free parking

VILLAGE FAIR
777 Bridgeway, Sausalito / 332-1902

Onetime Chinese gambling hall, opium den and bootleg distillery, Village Fair continues to thrive. Now a Mediterranean-style shopping center, the bazaar's current incarnation includes four levels of shops, cafes and boutiques set on a hillside that faces Sausalito Yacht Harbor and San Francisco Bay. Visitors can get pleasantly lost discovering an endless variety of imports, hand-crafted gifts, works of art and spectacular views.

Open daily

RESTAURANTS

ADRIANA'S RESTAURANT
999 Andersen Dr., San Rafael / 454-8000
Lunch Mon-Fri, dinner Mon-Sat
ITALIAN

The great food of Mill Valley's Giramonti can also be found in San Rafael, where diners enjoy the unsurpassed Italian home cooking of chef/owner Adriana Giramonti.

ALTA MIRA HOTEL RESTAURANT
125 Bulkley, Sausalito / 332-1350
Breakfast daily, lunch Mon-Sat, dinner daily, brunch Sun
CONTINENTAL

The Alta Mira has a sunny terrace for outdoor lunch and the immensely popular brunch and an elegant interior with a panoramic bay view for dinner.

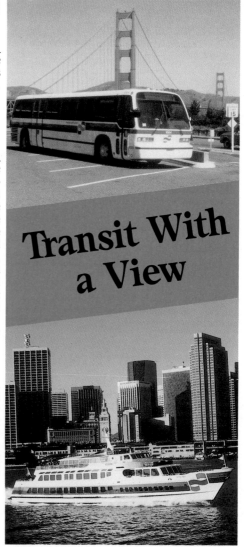

Transit With a View

Golden Gate Bus & Ferry System serving Sonoma, Marin and San Francisco.

Be part of Golden Gate Transit's
POLLUTION SOLUTION!
For fare and schedule information, please call **332-6600 • TDD 257-4554** &

MARIN

THE AVENUE GRILL
44 E. Blithedale Ave., Mill Valley / 388-6003
Dinner daily
AMERICAN

The Avenue Grill in the heart of Mill Valley is a lively restaurant, very popular with locals, serving "upbeat American" food with eclectic embellishments.

BUCKEYE ROADHOUSE
15 Shoreline Hwy., Mill Valley / 331-2600
Lunch Mon-Sat, dinner daily, brunch Sun
AMERICAN

Buckeye's boisterous tavern room and lively dining area with a massive river rock fireplace invite a gathering of family and friends, as does the all-American cuisine featuring fresh California produce and house-smoked meats and fish.

CAFFE TUTTI
12 El Portal, Sausalito / 332-0211
Breakfast, lunch & dinner daily
ITALIAN

With a beautifully presented selection of light fare, Caffe Tutti is a comfortable and casual place to eat at the dock of the bay.

CAIRO CAFE
411 Strawberry Village, Mill Valley / 389-1101
Lunch Tues-Sat, dinner Tues-Sun
EGYPTIAN

Established in 1987, the Cairo is the only Egyptian restaurant in the Bay Area. It's exotic and intimate, with live belly dancing on weekends. Among the vegetarian and meat dishes are stuffed grape leaves, falafel, and *midammis*, mashed fava beans with tahini and olive oil.

THE CAPRICE
2000 Paradise Dr., Tiburon / 435-3400
Lunch & dinner daily
CONTINENTAL

In a quiet spot away from downtown Tiburon, the Caprice is elegant and romantic, with a panoramic view of San Francisco and the Golden Gate Bridge.

CASA MADRONA
801 Bridgeway, Sausalito / 331-5888
Lunch Mon-Fri, dinner daily, brunch Sun
CONTEMPORARY AMERICAN

In the century-old Casa Madrona Hotel, with its spectacular view of Sausalito harbor and the bay, this restaurant features elegant dining in a relaxed atmosphere. Specializing in simple, innovative fare, Casa Madrona is recognized for the excellence of its wine list as well as its cuisine. It's a romantic spot to eat, day or night.
Specialties: *Pistachio-crusted Rack of Lamb with Morel Mushroom Jus; Peppered Pork Tenderloin with Crisp Polenta & Pineapple-Sage Demi-glaze; Grilled Rare Ahi Tuna with Sticky Rice, Artichokes & Red Onion Jam*

CHRISTOPHE
1919 Bridgeway, Sausalito / 332-9244
Dinner Tues-Sun
FRENCH

A romantic, charming restaurant at the northern end of Sausalito, Christophe serves French cuisine, which changes seasonally.

CHRISTOPHER'S
9 Main St., Tiburon / 435-4600
Dinner daily, brunch Sun
AMERICAN

If you want a superb view of San Francisco and a romantic setting, head for Christopher's.

COCONUTS
3001 Bridgeway, Sausalito / 331-7515
Breakfast & lunch daily, dinner Tues-Sat
CARIBBEAN

Floral aqua-and-pink tablecloths, palm tree motifs and friendly waitresses add to the charm of Sausalito's only Caribbean restaurant.

EL PASEO
17 Throckmorton St., Mill Valley / 388-0741
Dinner daily
FRENCH

El Paseo is highly recommended for a romantic evening or special occasion. The wine list is outstanding, with more than 40,000 bottles including rare French vintages.

GIRAMONTI RESTAURANT
655 Redwood Hwy., Mill Valley / 383-3000
Dinner Tues-Sun
ITALIAN

Exquisitely prepared entrees and cozy dining overlooking Shelter Bay make Giramonti one of the best dining experiences in Marin County.

GUAYMAS
5 Main St., Tiburon / 435-6300
Lunch Mon-Sat, dinner daily, brunch Sun
MEXICAN

Guaymas's waterfront setting offers panoramic views of San Francisco, two outdoor patios and a beautiful adobe dining room.

HORIZONS
558 Bridgeway, Sausalito / 331-3232
Lunch & dinner daily
CALIFORNIA

There's a marvelous view of San Francisco from this casual, window-filled restaurant.

IL FORNAIO CUCINA ITALIANA
223 Town Center, Corte Madera / 927-4400
Lunch Mon-Fri, dinner daily, brunch Sat & Sun
ITALIAN

With its terracotta floor, frescoed walls and lively

atmosphere, Il Fornaio is more like Italy than Marin. Enjoy spit-roasted meat and fish, pizzette and home-made pasta, indoors or outside on the piazza.

THE LARK CREEK INN
234 Magnolia Ave., Larkspur / 924-7766
Lunch Mon-Fri, dinner daily, brunch Sun
REGIONAL AMERICAN

This creekside restaurant surrounded by redwoods fea-tures the innovative cuisine of celebrity Chef Bradley Ogden. The restaurant's outdoor patio is perfect for warm-weather dining.

MARGARITAVILLE
1200 Bridgeway, Sausalito / 331-3226
Lunch & dinner daily
MEXICAN

Like its counterpart across the bay, Margaritaville cap-tures the essence of margarita culture: pitchers of exotic concoctions, a shaker of salt and great tropical fare.

PIAZZA D'ANGELO
22 Miller Ave., Mill Valley / 388-2000
Lunch & dinner daily, brunch Sat & Sun
ITALIAN

Piazza d'Angelo is one of Marin's liveliest spots — hip, swank and always bustling with energy. Specializing in regional Italian presentations, the restaurant uses orig-inal and seasonal ingredients, prepared with a light, refreshing Mediterranean-style taste. Seating is available in the villa-style garden, in the marble and terra-cotta trattoria, or in the dining room.
Specialties: Spaghetti alla Calabrese; Breast of Chicken with Artichoke Hearts, Fresh Tomatoes, Mushrooms, Oregano & White Wine; Pizza Quattro Stagione (Pizza with Prosciutto, Artichoke, Olives, Mushrooms & Anchovies); Rolled Scalloppine Filled with Prosciutto & Fontina Cheese

REMILLARD'S
125 E. Sir Francis Drake Blvd., Larkspur / 461-3700
Lunch Tues-Fri, dinner Tues-Sun, brunch Sun
FRENCH

Classic French cuisine at its best can be enjoyed in Marin's most unusual restaurant setting: a converted brick kiln built in 1891, with curving brick walls softly lit for romance and intimacy. Don't pass up the exquisite dessert souffles.
Specialties: Fresh Maine Lobster Wrapped in a Crepe with Nantois Sauce; Marinated Rack of Lamb with Bearnaise Sauce; Veal Sweetbreads with Braised Endive; Fresh Poached Salmon in Chive Sauce; Individual Dessert Souffles Prepared to Order

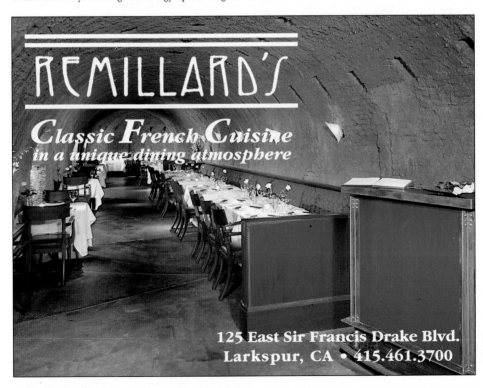

MARIN

RISTORANTE FABRIZIO
455 Magnolia Ave., Larkspur / 924-3332
Lunch Mon-Fri, dinner daily
ITALIAN

After working in San Francisco's finest Italian and French restaurants, Fabrizio Martinelli opened his own establishment in Marin County 12 years ago. Last fall, the restaurant unveiled a stunning new look with lots of natural light and subtle colors. Fabrizio also updated the menu. Light, health-conscious dishes, emphasizing pastas and seafood, complement traditional favorites. Fabrizio says he was inspired by trends in Italy where restaurants successfully blend old and new in both their cuisine and decor. Fabrizio continues to run a generous restaurant, paying special attention to every one of his customers. Affordable lunch specials include pasta and salad and an Italian sandwich with soup and salad. Fabrizio has a nonsmoking policy.
Specialties: Gnocchi Porcini: Tagliarini Verdi with Tomatoes & Prawns; Rigatoni in Vodka Sauce; Scalloppine of Chicken & Salmon with Lime Sauce

ROYAL THAI
610 3rd St., San Rafael / 485-1074
Lunch Mon-Fri, dinner daily
THAI

Spicy, perfectly balanced Thai food is served in a comfortably renovated old house in central San Rafael.

SAM'S ANCHOR CAFE
27 Main St., Tiburon / 435-4527
Lunch Mon-Fri, dinner daily, brunch Sat & Sun
AMERICAN

Seafood, hamburgers and omelettes served on a waterfront deck with a great view make Sam's a favorite spot.

SAVANNAH GRILL
55 Tamal Vista Blvd., Corte Madera / 924-6774
Lunch & dinner daily
AMERICAN

A large dining room accented by cherrywood, marble and brass has front-row counter seats for a young crowd that enjoys the cooking show in the open kitchen.

THE SPINNAKER
100 Spinnaker Dr., Sausalito / 332-1500
Lunch Mon-Sat, dinner daily, brunch Sun
SEAFOOD

Popular with both tourists and San Franciscans, the Spinnaker offers a great view of San Francisco, Alcatraz, the Marin Hills and Belvedere Peninsula.

STATION HOUSE CAFE
Main St., Point Reyes Station / 663-1515
Breakfast, lunch & dinner daily
AMERICAN

Right in the center of tiny Point Reyes Station, the cafe is a natural stop when you're visiting the area. The surprise is just how fresh and inventive the fare is.

WINSHIPS RESTAURANT
670 Bridgeway, Sausalito / 332-1454
Breakfast & lunch daily, dinner Wed-Sun
SEAFOOD

Located in downtown Sausalito, Winships serves fresh seafood and pasta in the town's oldest brick building, constructed in 1875.

ACCOMMODATIONS

CASA MADRONA HOTEL
801 Bridgeway, Sausalito / 332-0502

Nestled in a wooded Sausalito hillside overlooking the yacht harbor, Casa Madrona provides a serene, gardenlike escape into a private world of comfort. A certified historic landmark, the cascading structure flows down the hillside. It offers an elegant restaurant featuring American cuisine and a spectacular view. The hotel has 35 guest rooms and several cottages, many with fireplaces or wet bars. With its discreet, excellent service and romantic decor, Casa Madrona is a honeymooners' delight.
Singles & doubles $105-$185; suites $225

MOUNTAIN HOME INN
810 Panoramic Hwy., Mill Valley / 381-9000

Located on the slopes of Mt. Tamalpais, this luxury country inn is styled after Yosemite's Ahwahnee. Deluxe rooms have jacuzzis and fireplaces; some rooms have decks. Lunch and dinner are served Tuesday through Sunday at the **Mountain Home Inn**.

THE PELICAN INN
10 Pacific Way, Muir Beach / 383-6000

Located 20 minutes from the Golden Gate Bridge on Highway One one block from the ocean, The Pelican Inn is an authentic English bed-and-breakfast inn filled with antiques. English beers on tap are dispensed in the pub, lunch and dinner are offered in the dining room or on the terrace, and afternoon tea is served by the fire.

THE SAUSALITO HOTEL
16 El Portal, Sausalito / 332-4155

This charming 15-room bed-and-breakfast inn is a turn-of-the-century Victorian conveniently located near the Red & White Fleet ferry dock in the center of Sausalito.

THE TIBURON LODGE
1651 Tiburon Blvd., Tiburon / 435-3133

Suites with in-room spas, a large pool with patio and a downstairs coffee shop await your pleasure at this rustic-flavored hotel in the heart of Tiburon.

CALENDAR OF EVENTS

For specific dates, contact the Marin County Chamber of Commerce at 472-7470. For events in Sausalito, call the Sausalito Chamber of Commerce at 332-0505.

JANUARY

WHALE WATCHING
California gray whales migrate south to Baja during the winter months. The best viewing area in Marin is along the Point Reyes National Seashore.

FEBRUARY

MILL VALLEY FOOD FOR LOVERS
Area restaurants participate in a gourmet food festival in Mill Valley.

MARCH

EGRET AND BLUE HERON NESTING SEASON
The nesting season is from March through July, Audubon Canyon Ranch, Stinson Beach.

FAMILY DAYS AT SLIDE RANCH
A sample of life on a working farm. Activities include milking goats and baking bread, Slide Ranch at Muir Beach.

FARM DAY
Farm animals and farming demonstrations at the Farmers Market, Marin Center in San Rafael.

APRIL

YACHTING SEASON
The official opening of the yachting season is celebrated with decorated yachts and a ceremonial blessing. Events take place along the waterfront in Tiburon and Sausalito.

MAY

MILL VALLEY WEEKEND
A parade, picnics, crafts, an open studio tour, a walking tour and exhibits celebrate Mill Valley's history.

JUNE

SAUSALITO HUMMING TOADFISH FESTIVAL
The fish's nocturnal love call puzzled Sausalito's houseboat dwellers — and kept them awake — for some time before marine biologists detected its cause. Now, adversity has been turned into celebration. The humming toadfish is touted with a kazoo parade, humming contests and performances by comedians, jugglers and musicians at the Sausalito Bay Model.

SAN ANSELMO ART AND WINE FESTIVAL
San Anselmo's gourmet food, wine and art festival, nicknamed the "Function at the Junction." The event takes place along San Anselmo Avenue.

MILL VALLEY WINE FESTIVAL
Wine and food festival at Lytton Square, Mill Valley.

JULY

FOURTH OF JULY CELEBRATIONS
Bolinas celebrates Independence Day with a parade, foot races and a barbecue. Sausalito has a parade and a picnic. The town of Inverness marks the day with a parade, a barbecue and contests.

MARIN COUNTY FAIR
The county's biggest fair. Food, carnival rides and games, entertainment, special events and fireworks each night. The fair will feature a day of festivities on the Fourth of July, Marin County Fairgrounds in San Rafael.

SEPTEMBER

SAUSALITO ART FESTIVAL
Labor Day arts festival along Sausalito's waterfront. The weekend arts and crafts fair is the most popular event in Marin County.

RENAISSANCE PLEASURE FAIRE
Theme fair in Novato: the fair recreates an Elizabethan village with a royal court, jousting, food, entertainment and arts and crafts.

HARVEST FAIRE
Arts and crafts and fall produce fair at the Marin County Fairgrounds, San Rafael.

OCTOBER

SUNNY HILLS GRAPE FESTIVAL
Entertainment, music, puppet shows, handcrafted items and homemade foods at the Larkspur Landing Shopping Center, Larkspur.

MILL VALLEY FILM FESTIVAL
One of Northern California's major film festivals. Special events, film tributes and new films by American and foreign film directors are presented at the Sequoia Theatre, Mill Valley.

ACORN FESTIVAL
Marin County's indigenous Miwok Indians are honored at a fall festival, Point Reyes National Seashore.

NOVEMBER

HOLIDAY CRAFTS FAIRE
Holiday gifts at the Marin Center, San Rafael.

DECEMBER

LIGHTED YACHT PARADE
A parade of yachts lit for the holidays, Sausalito waterfront.

PARADE OF LIGHTS
Holiday candlelight procession, San Rafael.

BOLINAS CHRISTMAS CRAFT FAIR
Arts and crafts holiday fair presented by artists in West Marin, Bolinas.

MARIN